STUDIES IN HISTORY, ECONOMICS AND
PUBLIC LAW

Edited by the
FACULTY OF POLITICAL SCIENCE
OF COLUMBIA UNIVERSITY

Number 466

THE AMERICAN DEPARTMENT OF THE
BRITISH GOVERNMENT, 1768–1782

BY

MARGARET MARION SPECTOR

# THE
# AMERICAN DEPARTMENT
## OF THE
# BRITISH GOVERNMENT
## 1768-1782

BY

MARGARET MARION SPECTOR

OCTAGON BOOKS

A DIVISION OF FARRAR, STRAUS AND GIROUX

New York    1976

Copyright 1940 by Columbia University Press

*Reprinted 1976*
*by special arrangement with Columbia University Press*

OCTAGON BOOKS
A DIVISION OF FARRAR, STRAUS & GIROUX, INC.
19 Union Square West
New York, N.Y. 10003

Library of Congress Cataloging in Publication Data

Spector, Margaret Marion Mitchell, 1904-
    The American Department of the British Government, 1768-1782.

    Reprint of the ed. published by Columbia University Press, New York, which was issued as no. 466 of Studies in history, economics, and public law.
    Thesis—Columbia University, 1940.
    Vita.
    Bibliography: p.
    Includes index.
    1. Great Britain. Secretary of State for the American or Colonial Department.  2. Great Britain—Colonies—Administration.  3. Great Britain—Politics and government—1760-1789.  I. Title.  II. Series: Columbia studies in the social sciences; 466.

JV1043.S7   1976             325'.31'0941           76-25085
ISBN 0-374-97535-3

Manufactured by Braun-Brumfield, Inc.
Ann Arbor, Michigan
Printed in the United States of America

To

My Parents

JAMES EDWARD AND MARGARET MITCHELL

# CONTENTS

|  | PAGE |
|---|---|
| PREFACE | 9 |

### CHAPTER I
The Origin of the American Department . . . . . . . . . . . . . . . 11

### CHAPTER II
The Status of the American Department . . . . . . . . . . . . . . . 25

### CHAPTER III
Organization and Personnel . . . . . . . . . . . . . . . . . . . . . 33

### CHAPTER IV
Salaries, Fees, and Emoluments . . . . . . . . . . . . . . . . . . . 48

### CHAPTER V
The Feud with the "Ancient" Secretaries . . . . . . . . . . . . . . 66

### CHAPTER VI
Relations with Other Departments . . . . . . . . . . . . . . . . . . 79

### CHAPTER VII
Biographical Sketches of the Under-Secretaries . . . . . . . . . . 100

### CHAPTER VIII
The Colonial Office Correspondence . . . . . . . . . . . . . . . . 111

### CHAPTER IX
The Under-Secretary and Colonial Policy . . . . . . . . . . . . . . 136

### CHAPTER X
The Abolition of the American Department . . . . . . . . . . . . . 159

BIBLIOGRAPHY . . . . . . . . . . . . . . . . . . . . . . . . . . . . 169
INDEX . . . . . . . . . . . . . . . . . . . . . . . . . . . . . . . 177

# PREFACE

THIS work is the direct outgrowth of a study of William Knox, permanent Under-secretary in the American Department, 1770-1782, upon which the writer has been engaged for several years. In her study of Knox the author was soon confronted with the lack of any comprehensive work on the American or Colonial Department in which he served. A. H. Basye's valuable article on "The Secretary of State for the Colonies" (*American Historical Review*, XXVIII, 13-23, October, 1922) covers only one phase of the present work. It throws no light on the organization, personnel, and financial set-up of the department or on the responsibilities of the Under-secretaries. Likewise, Mark Thomson in *The Secretaries of State, 1681-1782* (Oxford, 1932) necessarily devotes but a few pages to the American Secretaries. The writer has therefore deemed it advisable to present the available facts about the American Department in the belief that such a study would make a further contribution to the history of British politics in the age of the American Revolution.

This monograph is a study of the origin, organization, and functioning of the department which, from 1768 to 1782, was responsible for the administration of the colonies and which was largely responsible for the conduct of the American war. Special emphasis has been placed on the personality, work, and influence of the Under-secretaries, in particular, John Pownall and William Knox, who have been almost completely ignored heretofore. It will be obvious to the reader that this work does not pretend to be another history of British colonial policy.

As the bibliography and the footnotes following the several chapters indicate, the present study is based chiefly upon research in widely scattered collections of primary sources, both manuscript and printed. References to the American Department in secondary sources are, in the main, fragmentary and incidental. Only those books which have a direct bearing on some phase of this work have been included in the bibliography.

## PREFACE

The writer takes this opportunity to thank the staffs of the Public Record Office, British Museum, Canadian Archives, and William L. Clements Library for their active and cheerful coöperation during the examination of the major primary sources. In particular, some acknowledgment must be made of the courtesy and hospitality of the late Earl of Dartmouth who permitted the examination of relevant materials in the Dartmouth Manuscripts at Patshull House. The writer was likewise given access to the Sackville Manuscripts remaining at Drayton by Major Nigel Stopford Sackville. Captain H. V. Knox of Oxford willingly placed a small collection of private papers of William Knox at the writer's disposal. In addition to the permission granted by Dr. Randolph G. Adams for the use of the facilities of the Clements Library, the late Mr. William L. Clements generously permitted the author to examine the Sackville and Clinton Manuscripts at his home in Bay City, Michigan. A special debt of gratitude is due to Professor R. L. Schuyler of Columbia University for his unfailing patience in guiding the author during the preparation of the manuscript. Professor J. B. Brebner of Columbia University recommended the separation of this study of the American Department from the original work on William Knox. This list of acknowledgments would not be complete without some tribute to the Canadian Federation of University Women, whose traveling fellowship was held by the author, 1934-35, thereby making possible the completion of the greater part of her research abroad. Last, but not least, the writer is indebted to her husband, Professor Ivar Spector of the University of Washington, for numerous hints and suggestions during the final reorganization of the manuscript.

M. S.

SEATTLE, AUGUST 15, 1939.

# CHAPTER I
# THE ORIGIN OF THE AMERICAN DEPARTMENT

THE first British Empire reached maturity without the guidance of a colonial secretary and a colonial department. The functions of the Board of Trade, established in 1696, were those of investigating and advising upon colonial affairs rather than administering them. Not until 1768, at a time when the first Empire was threatened with disintegration, was a colonial or American department established in the British Government. The new department was destined to function under the abnormal conditions of crisis and revolution, and to be manned by officials who had little or no understanding of colonial psychology, until it was finally abolished in 1782 when the American colonies had virtually attained their independence. Although the Colonial Department contributed nothing to the building of the Empire, and although it failed to prevent the revolt of the colonies, it occupied a strategic position during the American Revolution, the course of which it helped more than a little to determine.

In 1764, when Thomas Pownall, former Governor of Massachusetts Bay, first published his *Administration of the Colonies*, he severely criticized the division of responsibility for colonial measures among the various departments of the British Government and strongly recommended the delegation of undivided authority to one department under a secretary of state for the colonies.[1] There was some justice in Pownall's arraignment of the old régime in imperial administration. When he wrote, the colonies fell directly, although not exclusively, under the supervision of the Secretary of State for the Southern Department, who was also responsible for French, Swiss, Italian, Spanish, Turkish, and Irish affairs, for the Channel Islands, and for an undefined share of domestic business.[2] The King, the Privy Council, Parliament, the Treasury with its subordinate boards and officials, the Paymaster-General of the Forces, the Admiralty with its sundry branches, the War Office, and the Board of Trade and Plantations were all in one way or another concerned with colonial affairs.[3] There was no one individual or department primarily responsible for the coördination of the efforts of these various branches of administration. In 1766 the Earl of Chesterfield gloomily reflected that "if we have no Secretary of State with full and undisputed powers for America, in a few years we may as well have no America."[4]

Although there had never existed a department of state for colonial administration, there were precedents enough to warrant the establishment of a third secretaryship.[5] Theoretically the Secretariat was one and indivisible, but in practice there had been since the time of Henry VIII at least two Secretaries, sometimes three, and on one occasion possibly four. The first case of the appointment of a Third Secretary occurred in 1553, during the last year of the reign of Edward VI, when the political maneuvers of the Duke of Northumberland were probably responsible for the appointment of Sir John Cheke as the colleague of Sir William Petre and Sir William Cecil. The experiment was repeated in 1616-17, when James I had three Secretaries, Sir John Herbert, Sir Ralph Wynood, and Sir Thomas Lake.

Queen Anne, on the pretext that business was increasing, appointed the Duke of Queensbury Third Secretary in 1709. He and his successors, although their appointments in no way differed from those of their colleagues, were, for all practical purposes, Secretaries for Scottish affairs and seldom interfered in matters pertaining solely to England.[6] They were excluded from foreign affairs, although they enjoyed the same salary, board wages, and secret service funds as the other two Secretaries. Even this failed to satisfy Queensbury, for he demanded, apparently without success, an equal share of the fees of office.[7] The dispute between Queensbury and his colleagues foreshadows the later and more frequent clashes between the

THE ORIGIN OF THE AMERICAN DEPARTMENT 13

American Secretaries and those for the Southern and Northern Departments.[8] During the absence of Stanhope from the Southern Department in 1716, Sir Paul Methuen received a regular appointment as Secretary of State and remained in office for a short time after Stanhope's return.[9] In 1723, when Townshend and Carteret were both absent, their places were filled by the Duke of Roxborough and Robert Walpole, the last mentioned becoming to all intents and purposes a fourth Secretary.[10] With the resignation of the Marquis of Tweeddale, the last Secretary for Scotland, in 1746, these sporadic attempts to establish a third secretaryship definitely lapsed, and from that time until the appointment of the Earl of Hillsborough in 1768 there were only two Secretaries of State, one for the Southern and the other for the Northern Department. It is perhaps worth noting here that the peculiar division of foreign and the sharing of domestic business between the Northern and Southern Secretaries, a procedure not followed elsewhere in Europe, frequently led to friction between them during the eighteenth century.

Thomas Pownall was not the first person to become conscious of the need for a distinct colonial department, although he may well have been the first to consign his recommendations to print. The ambitious Lord Halifax, far from being satisfied with the presidency of the Board of Trade, where he complained that he was treated as a wretch and a nobody, would gladly have elevated himself to the post of Secretary for the Plantations. To achieve his ends he enlisted the services of the Duke of Newcastle in 1751. He complained to Newcastle that the other departments had not only usurped a considerable proportion of the Board's patronage, but that they assumed that the Board could make recommendations on colonial issues only when its advice was specially requested.[11] He asked for a seat in the Cabinet with access to the King. The Duke of Bedford, who viewed these negotiations with a jaundiced eye, warned George II that Newcastle and Halifax were plotting behind his back to "lop off" the American business from the Southern Department with the intention of assigning it to Halifax as First Lord of Trade.[12]

The consequent refusal of his demands did not deter Halifax from trying again. In December he asked for the right to attend Cabinet meetings when colonial affairs were under discussion and demanded that the Board be given control of such patronage as did not fall to the Admiralty and the Treasury.[13] Apparently Halifax would have been satisfied with the direction of the West Indies, but the Earl of Holderness, Secretary for the Southern Department, bitterly and it seems effectually, protested against the plucking of what he considered the best feather in his cap.[14] A compromise was effected by an order-in-council of March 11, 1752, which effectively strengthened the Board of Trade as far as colonial patronage was concerned, although it did not concede the sum total of Halifax's demands.[15] His request to participate in Cabinet discussion of colonial issues was granted.

In the interests of ambition and efficiency, Halifax, in 1757, urged his appointment as secretary of state for the colonies. It may have been at this time that he submitted his observations on the manner of appointing a third secretary and on the emoluments of the office.[16] Newcastle capitulated during the involved negotiations preparatory to the forming of the Pitt-Newcastle coalition, but neglected to inform Pitt of the proposed change.[17] This proved fatal to the whole scheme, for Pitt promptly vetoed any further encroachment by the Board of Trade on the Southern Department. Halifax, although he at first resigned in a huff, had to be content with his old office plus a seat in the Cabinet granted to him, not as President of the Board, but as Earl of Halifax.[18] His strenuous efforts to secure the post of third secretary had failed, and when he resigned in 1761 Pitt succeeded in depriving the Board of its right to make recommendations for colonial appointments.[19]

If subsequent maneuvers for the establishment of a colonial department are to be understood, some reference must be made

THE ORIGIN OF THE AMERICAN DEPARTMENT 15

here to the political situation which confronted George III upon his accession in 1760.[20] During the reign of George II, the Whigs, under the leadership of Walpole and Pelham, had built up a powerful political machine, based in part at least, on the distribution of patronage and the control of elections. Party lines, however, were not yet clearly defined and there were Whigs both in and out of office. The members of the Opposition, which consisted chiefly of those deprived of office, gravitated in the direction of Leicester House, the home of the heir to the throne, upon whose accession their political future depended. The Tories, still suffering from the stigma of Jacobitism, were for the most part leaderless, although in the later years of the reign of George II some of them supported Pitt. Thus politics, as L. B. Namier points out, tended to become little more than a conflict between successive generations.[21] Due to the longevity of George II, many of the hangers-on of Leicester House grew old before they had any opportunity to taste the fruits of office.

Under these circumstances, it would have been logical for George III to replace his grandfather's supporters with his own followers immediately after his accession in 1760. Political exile, however, had not served to prepare either the Leicester House clique or the Tories for leadership, and the Seven Years' War continued. For the time being, George III had to be content with the addition of the Earl of Bute to the Cabinet. Even the Duke of Newcastle, distributer of political patronage for George II, retained his post at the Treasury to manage the election of 1761 by methods similar to those he had utilized in the past. The truce with Newcastle proved to be of short duration. When his system collapsed under the strain of the peace negotiations, George III proceeded to adapt the Whig machine to his own purposes. For some years the lack of suitable leadership handicapped his efforts to create a stable court faction. Bute, Grenville, Rockingham, and even Pitt were tried and in one way or another found wanting.

The decade between 1760 and 1770 witnessed a remarkable change in political personnel, owing to the death or retirement of men like Lord Melcombe (Dodington), Egremont, Hardwicke, Bath, Cumberland, Charles Townshend, Newcastle, Grenville, Charles Yorke, etc. At the time of Newcastle's death in 1768, only two-fifths of the members of the House of Commons had served prior to the accession of George III. By 1770, according to Namier, the political leaders of 1760, with the exception of Chatham and Sandwich, were no longer active in the political arena.[22] Events proved, too, that the power of men like Newcastle and Grenville depended more on office than on principles. Out of office their followers not only dwindled in number, but many joined the ranks of the rising court faction. Many former Grenvillites, including Weyburn, Suffolk, Wedderburn, and Thurlow, later found lucrative posts in the North administration.

George III put the finishing touch to his political edifice when in 1770 he found his Newcastle in the person of Lord North, a nephew of the ambitious Halifax and an apprentice in the Newcastle régime.[23] Having taken over the political machine of his predecessor, George III was able to use it effectively until he and his so-called Tory followers [24] were confronted with military defeat in the American Revolution. When in 1780 the Opposition Whigs demanded the overthrow of the King's system, they were, curiously enough, attacking the machine created by their own party under George II.[25]

In view of the conditions outlined above, it was only natural that the idea of creating a colonial department, with the patronage attached thereto, afforded one reasonably sound method of increasing the influence of the Court faction during the years that followed the accession of George III. It is significant that Bute, in an attempt to save his tottering administration, offered Charles Townshend the post of colonial secretary as early as 1762. Townshend, however, bluntly refused to have anything to do with the Bute régime, much to the astonishment of Henry Fox, who somewhat prematurely congratulated him on the appointment.[26] For the next five years, plans for the establishment of a colonial department recurred with each projected change in the administration. Had efficiency in government been the primary motive in the minds of the advocates of such a move, the proposal of Halifax for the elevation of the Board of Trade to a Secretaryship could have eliminated the duplication of offices involved in the creation of another department. As it was, the King, by setting up a separate American or Colonial Department in 1768, effectively strengthened his own position. In the minds of Burke, Fox, and other opponents of George III, the department therefore represented an important cog in the King's system. Because of these circumstances, coincidence alone can scarcely account for the fact that the abolition of the American Department in 1782 occurred simultaneously with a powerful frontal attack on all that the King's system represented.

No doubt Pownall's recommendations in 1764 impressed some ministers with the advisability of erecting a colonial department. Hillsborough, an adherent of the Court faction, and Dartmouth seem to have heeded his warning that America would never take England seriously until an efficient system of administration was adopted. In 1765, when some change in the status of the Board of Trade was under consideration, Hillsborough assured Dartmouth that the acceptance of anything short of the authority wielded by the Treasury and Admiralty in their respective departments would bring him continual disappointment and perhaps undeserved disgrace.[27]

The Rockingham ministry seriously contemplated the creation of a colonial department in the spring of 1766, both in the interests of efficiency and as a part of the reorganization necessary to stabilize the administration. The Newcastle Manuscripts in the British Museum contain two plans for the rearrangement of the Cabinet, one proposing Charles Townshend, the other the Earl of Dartmouth, as "Third Secretary of State for America."[28] In the case of Townshend it was proposed to raise him to the peerage, no doubt with the intention of avoiding embarrassing questions in the House of Commons about the operation of the Place Acts of Queen Anne.[29] The Duke of Richmond, who was eventually selected for the Southern Department, was entirely in sympathy with the plan to partition his office, " having often heard that the American affairs load the Southern Department with so much business, as to make it almost impossible to go through with it." [30] Newcastle was of the same opinion,[31] but he seems to have entertained a wholesome respect for the Place Acts.

Although Townshend again refused the position, Dartmouth proved more placable. For some time, however, the Ministry wavered between his appointment as third secretary and the less radical expedient of retaining him as First Lord of Trade with the powers formerly wielded by Halifax.[32] The Earl of Chesterfield urged him to put aside his " natural timidity and diffidence," to strike while the iron was hot for dignity as well as power, and to accept nothing less than the post of Secretary of State with " all the forms and privileges of that office." [33] Before any decision could be reached, negotiations for the return of Pitt to power effectually terminated the discussion.[34] Pitt had consistently opposed the partition of the Southern Department. On July 25, 1766, Rockingham notified Dartmouth that the King did not approve that part of the plan which contemplated the amalgamation of a separate colonial department with the Board of Trade.[35] Dartmouth preferred to resign rather than to accept an inferior post at the Board. Hillsborough succeeded him, and Shelburne became the Secretary of State for the Southern Department.

After this second failure to transform the Board of Trade into a department of state, the Government resorted to Pownal's alternative suggestion of reducing it to a mere board of reference, at the same time concentrating all power and authority in the hands of the Southern Secretary.[36] Hillsborough, although he still regarded an independent department as " most desirable for the public," was convinced that those who held the patronage would make such a departure impossible. He therefore accepted the Board of Trade with the intention of transferring every vestige of executive power and patronage to Shelburne's office.[37] Having washed his hands of any consequences that might result from this expedient, and following his natural bent to make things "easy for himself," he proved even more willing to surrender his authority than Shelburne was to receive it.[38] The remainder of the order-in-council of March, 1752, which instructed colonial Governors to correspond with the Board, and to resort to the Secretary of State only in urgent matters, was now rescinded. Had the Southern Department been solely, or even primarily concerned with colonial affairs, the new arrangement might have achieved the same purpose as the elevation of the Board into a separate department. As it was, this *modus vivendi* did not last long.

The weakness and instability of the administration after Chatham's collapse led to renewed attempts to stabilize it in 1767 by the appointment of a colonial secretary. In April, two plans were proposed, both of which included the Earl of Dartmouth as third secretary for America.[39] Shelburne soon found himself at variance with his colleagues, who were not averse to reducing his power by the partition of his office. In July and August, during an attempt to reconcile the conflicting interests of General Conway and George Grenville, the division of the Southern Department was discussed behind Shelburne's back. To retain Conway's support in the House of Commons, the King offered him an appointment as "Secretary of State for America." The plan was discarded after the Attorney-General expressed the opinion that no member of the House of Commons could occupy such a post on account of the Place Acts.[40] The Duke of Grafton, the nominal head of the administration, then flirted with the possibility of relieving the political tension by an alliance with the Bedfordites. He boldly asserted that neither a Solomon nor a horse could manage the business of the Southern Department satisfactorily, and as on several previous occasions he pronounced himself in favor of partition.[41]

In December, Grafton broached the subject of partition to Shelburne, proposing that he retain the conduct of American affairs. After two interviews Shelburne reluctantly acquiesced in the division of his office, not from conviction, but largely for the sake of Chatham and because Grafton insisted that there was no alternative.[42] Shelburne was unable to obtain an opinion on the partition from Chatham. Left entirely to his own devices, he preferred to retain the Southern Department because he was loath to assume the difficult task of " framing and modelling " a new office.[43] By Christmas the Grafton-Bedford alliance was complete, and the Earl of Hillsborough, an adherent of the Court faction, was chosen Secretary of State for America. The actual changes did not take place until January, 1768.[44]

The creation of the Colonial or American Department was obviously the result of maneuvers for the restoration of political equilibrium. The Irishman's reason assigned by Edmund Burke in 1780, that two Secretaries were doing nothing and therefore a third was appointed to help them, was not a very profound analysis of the situation.[45] Burke and Walpole were nearer the truth in claiming that the department was established to consolidate the King's influence. One critic of the King's system, perhaps wise after the event, asserted that the establishment of a department of state for America led by Hillsborough presaged the adoption of " extraordinary measures " against the colonies, where, he says, the step caused a general alarm.[46] Contemporary sources seem to provide little basis to support the contention that the department was created for the purpose of suppressing opposition in the colonies. Actually, its establishment appears to have had more immediate effects upon English politics than upon colonial policy. In so far as its advent represented a triumph for the King's system, however, there could be little hope for a policy of toleration and liberality when colonial controversies occurred.

The correspondence relative to the genesis of the department reveals in the minds of those who were responsible for its estab-

THE ORIGIN OF THE AMERICAN DEPARTMENT 21

lishment only a secondary concern for the improvement of imperial administration. That is particularly true in the case of Hillsborough who became the first incumbent of the office. In Halifax, personal ambition was so confused with the demand for efficient administration that it is difficult to distinguish which was paramount. Men like Grafton seem to have used the argument of executive efficiency to justify the rather dubious political alignments which were being sought at the time. A colonial department, created in response to the political machinations of the moment, augured ill for the successful functioning of imperial organization. There was some reason to believe that those who visualized such a department as a pawn in the game of politics would continue to regard it as such after its establishment. There can be no doubt, however, that the co-ordination of colonial business in the hands of one department was the most desirable method of dealing with American problems. The organization and operation of that department now demand our attention.

1 Thomas Pownall, *Administration of the Colonies* (1st ed., London, 1764), pp. 11-20. Pownall suggested that this could be done either by the creation of a new department or by elevating the Board of Trade to a department of state.

2 See Mark Thomson, *The Secretaries of State, 1681-1782* (Oxford, 1932), chaps. iii and iv. In theory the Secretariat was indivisible and the Secretary for the Northern Department could and did deal with colonial affairs. This rarely happened after the creation of the Board of Trade in 1696, except in the absence of the Southern Secretary.

3 See C. M. Andrews, *The Colonial Background of the American Revolution* (New Haven, 1935), chap. ii; O. M. Dickerson, *American Colonial Government, 1696-1765* (Cleveland, 1912), chaps. ii and iii.

4 *Hist. MSS Comm., Dartmouth MSS* (London, 1896), III, 182, Chesterfield to Dartmouth, May 24, 1766.

5 These precedents are discussed in F. S. Thomas, *Notes of Materials for the History of Public Departments* (London, 1846), pp. 26-7. See also *Parliamentary History* (London, 1806-20), XX, 250 *et seq.*, " Debate on the Right of Lord George Germain (as Third Secretary of State) to sit in the House of Commons," March 11, 1779. Shelburne also collected material on the subject. See Shelburne MSS, Vol. 134.

6 For the Third Secretary for Scotland, see Thomson, *op. cit.*, chap. i, pp. 29-38; Brit. Mus., Harleian MSS, Vol. 2263, f. 338; Stowe MSS, Vol.

163, f. 161. The warrant for his appointment stated that "the public business of this Her Majesty's kingdom increasing, Her Majesty is graciously pleased to constitute James Duke of Queensbury and Dover one of Her Majesty's Principal Secretaries, besides those now in being, during her Majesty's pleasure."

7 Shelburne MSS, Vol. 134, ff. 189-191, "Memorial about the Third Secretary of State, 1709"; and the reply, *ibid.*, ff. 195-98.

8 See *infra*, chap. v.

9 *Hist. MSS Comm., Polwarth MSS* (London, 1910), I, 35; W. M. Coxe, *Memoirs of Walpole* (3 vols., London, 1800), II, 155-6.

10 *Parliamentary History*, XX, 267. Thomas De Grey, Jr., in the House of Commons, stated that there were four Secretaries in 1723, the Duke of Roxborough, Sir Robert Walpole, and two others.

11 Brit. Mus., Add. MSS, 32725, f. 160, Newcastle to Halifax, September 10, 1751.

12 P. C. Yorke, *The Life and Correspondence of Philip Yorke Earl of Hardwicke*... (Cambridge, 1913), II, 116, Hardwicke to Newcastle, August 13, 1751.

13 Brit. Mus., Add. MSS, 32994, ff. 286-87; also A. H. Basye, *The Lords Commissioners of Trade and Plantations* (New Haven, 1925), p. 69.

14 Brit. Mus., Add. MSS, 35335, f. 62, Holderness to Newcastle, January 30, 1752.

15 *Acts of the Privy Council, Colonial Series* (London, 1912), IV, 4, 154-5; Brit. Mus., Add. MSS, 33029, f. 124.

16 Brit. Mus., Add. MSS, 33030, ff. 295-96, "Considerations on the Appointment of a Secretary of State." This may, however, have been written in 1767 when the appointment of a third secretary was again seriously considered. It is included with other letters of the year 1767.

17 G. B. Dodington, *Diary* (Salisbury, 1784), p. 396, April 6, 1757.

18 Brit. Mus., Add. MSS, 32997, f. 286, September 23, 1757. Hardwicke also favored this scheme. See Yorke, *Hardwicke*, II, 407-09, Hardwicke to Newcastle, June 25, 1757.

19 *Acts of the Privy Council, Colonial Series*, IV, 157.

20 For further details consult the excellent works of L. B. Namier, namely, *The Structure of Politics at the Accession of George III* (2 vols., London, 1929) and *England in the Age of the American Revolution* (London, 1930).

21 Namier, *England in the Age of the American Revolution*, p. 62.

22 *Ibid.*, p. 70.

23 See W. B. Pemberton, *Lord North* (London, 1938) for a recent biography of the Prime Minister. Although it is understood that Lord North was not a Prime Minister in the modern sense, it has been found convenient, for lack of a better term, to refer to him as such.

24 Namier says: "With the change of owners the building changed its name, and the Government party was now called 'Tory' by its opponents, and still continues to be described as such by some historians; but nothing can be more confusing than the application of the same name to bodies

THE ORIGIN OF THE AMERICAN DEPARTMENT 23

so widely differing in character and principles as the Tories of 1760 and the so-called Tories of 1780." *England in the Age of the American Revolution,* p. 219.

25 For the abolition of the Colonial Department, see chap. x.

26 W. S. Taylor and J. H. Pringle (eds.), *Chatham Correspondence* (London, 1838), II, 181-83, Thomas Nuthall to Lady Chatham, October 14, 1762.

27 *Hist. MSS Comm., Dartmouth MSS* (London, 1896), III, 179, Hillsborough to Dartmouth, September, 1765.

28 Brit. Mus., Add. MSS, 33001, f. 225, " Plan Taken Down by My Lord Rockingham, May 12, 1766"; *ibid.,* f. 227, " Plan Proposed This Day by My Lord Rockingham to the King, and agreed to by his Majesty, May 14, 1766."

29 Particularly the Act of 6 Anne, c. 7, which excluded those who accepted offices created after the passing of the Act from seats in the House of Commons, limited the number of Commissioners appointed to execute any office, and excluded from the House all who held pensions from the Crown during pleasure.

30 George Thomas, Earl of Albemarle (ed.), *Rockingham Memoirs* (London, 1852), I, 341-43, Duke of Richmond to Rockingham, May 19, 1766.

31 Brit. Mus., Add. MSS, 32975, ff. 104-05, Newcastle to Conway, May 7, 1766; " No one man can have the time to do the duty of Secretary of State and attend the King every day and give that attention to the settlement and government of our colonies, which in their present situation they will require."

32 W. J. Smith (ed.), *Grenville Papers* (London, 1853), III, 235, Whately to Grenville, May 23, 1766. Whately also reports Townshend's refusal, p. 236.

33 *Hist. MSS Comm., Dartmouth MSS,* III, 182, Chesterfield to Dartmouth, May 24, 1766.

34 Pitt had opposed the measure in 1757. See Basil Williams, *Earl of Chatham* (London, 1913), II, 214 n., where it is stated that Pitt contemplated such a step in 1766 after he entered office.

35 *Hist. MSS Comm., Dartmouth MSS,* III, 182, Rockingham to Dartmouth, July 25, 1766.

36 Pownall, *op. cit.,* p. 20.

37 *Grenville Papers,* III, 294-96, Hillsborough to Grenville, August 6, 1766.

38 Shelburne MSS, Vol. 134, f. 73, Hillsborough to Shelburne, August 25, 1766; *ibid.,* f. 81, Shelburne to Hillsborough, August 26, 1766.

39 Brit. Mus., Add. MSS, 33001, f. 382, " Two Plans of Administration proposed to preserve an Equality in Either Plan," April 24, 1767.

40 J. B. Fortescue (ed.), *Correspondence of George III* (London, 1927-28), I, 500, King to Hertford, July 17, 1767; Horace Walpole, *Memoirs of George III* (London, 1894), III, 98-9. Grafton referred to these negotiations later in his interviews with Shelburne. See Lord Fitzmaurice, *Life of William, Earl of Shelburne* (London, 1912), I, 327.

**41** For these negotiations, see Walpole, *op. cit.*, III, 138-39. The Bedford group insisted on removing Shelburne from at least half his department. See also Fitzmaurice, *op. cit.*, I, chap. viii. Shelburne had two interviews with Grafton of which he left an account. *Cf.* Shelburne's letter to the Countess of Chatham, December 13, 1767, in the *Chatham Correspondence*, III, 298-302.

**42** *Chatham Correspondence*, III, 298-302.

**43** *Ibid.*, p. 299, Shelburne to Grafton, December 13, 1767.

**44** Mrs. Paget Toynbee (ed.), *The Letters of Horace Walpole* (16 vols., Oxford, 1903-05), VII, No. 1197, Walpole to Sir Horace Mann, December 25, 1767: "The Treaty is concluded. Shelburne keeps the Southern Department but Lord Hillsborough is Secretary of State for America."

**45** *Parliamentary History*, XXI, 205, "Debate on the abolition of the Colonial Department," March 8, 1780.

**46** *Anecdotes of the Life of the Right Hon. William Pitt, Earl of Chatham* (London, 1792), I, 351-52 (note).

## CHAPTER II

## THE STATUS OF THE AMERICAN DEPARTMENT

THE establishment of the American Department in 1768 occasioned surprisingly little comment on either side of the Atlantic. References in letters, diaries, and printed materials are too few in number to indicate the reaction of public opinion in England or America. The very dearth of such comments, however, is in itself indicative of the fact that the creation of the Colonial Department failed to make a very deep impression even on those it most concerned. On the whole, the new office evoked more criticism than praise. Those who disapproved the venture were inclined to look down upon the American Department as inferior to the Southern and Northern Departments. There was a tendency to regard it as a new office which could not be directed by a member of the House of Commons on account of the Place Acts. A few extremists believed the appointment of the Third Secretary to be illegal, or at least inexpedient. The skeptics merely waited to see with what degree of energy and efficiency the department would be managed. Even Americans do not seem to have derived any satisfaction from the co-ordination of colonial affairs. Benjamin Franklin, who was sufficiently representative, was openly suspicious of the motives and policies of the first incumbent of the office, the Earl of Hillsborough.[1] William Samuel Johnson, agent for Connecticut, cast another side-light on American reaction when he lamented the " unhappy delay " this reorganization would cause in the transaction of colonial business.[2]

What seems to have been the chief recognition of the Colonial Office in print came in the form of an anonymous pamphlet, entitled, *The First Measures Necessary to be Taken in the American Department*.[3] Its author, obviously a man with wide business interests, complained vigorously and not without some justification, of the great expense of " a new establishment which renders the old one [the Board of Trade] an expensive nothing."⁴ He was firmly convinced that the routine business could have been conducted by the subalterns in the Board of Trade, thereby avoiding this unnecessary duplication of offices. It seems unfortunate that the American Department failed to secure more co-operation from liberal-minded Englishmen or Americans at the time of its inauguration.

The manner of appointing the Third Secretary probably gave rise to the impression that the American Department was distinctly inferior to the Northern and Southern Departments. The regular method of appointing a secretary of state was by the issue of letters patent and delivery of the seals of office.⁵ In the case of the Third Secretary for Scotland, the warrant recorded the expediency of the step, but made no attempt to restrict his sphere of action.⁶ The manner of appointing a colonial secretary had been the subject of some consideration between Halifax and Newcastle. Halifax was of the opinion that one of two methods should be adopted: either an order-in-council should be passed setting forth the reasons for the change and directing a patent to be issued and seals prepared; or a Privy Council minute, following the precedent of the Scottish Secretaries, should explain that the increase of plantation business and the advantages anticipated from the adoption of one uniform method made it expedient to appoint a third secretary.⁷ His recommendations were not followed in 1768. Hillsborough's appointment was essentially the same as that of any other Secretary of State with the exception of the preamble of his commission which declared that " whereas the publick business of our colonies and plantations increasing, it seemeth expedient to us to appoint one other principal Secretary of State besides our two ancient Secretaries. . . ." ⁸

The inclusion of this preamble provided an opportunity for the opponents of the office to assert that the sphere of action of the Third Secretary was limited to the colonies, and that he was, therefore, in a position distinctly inferior to that of his two colleagues. The patents of the other two Secretaries

THE STATUS OF THE AMERICAN DEPARTMENT 27

in no way defined the scope of their activities. The King assigned to one the Southern and to the other the Northern Department, but each could, and frequently did, perform the functions of the other, while much of the domestic business was shared indiscriminately.

There is no doubt but that the Third Secretary was appointed with the specific intention of delegating to him all business relating at least to the American Colonies. Both before and after its establishment, the department was commonly referred to as "the American Department," and its chief as "Secretary of State for the Colonies" or "Third Secretary of State for America."[9] During the negotiations that preceded Hillsborough's appointment, however, there seems to have been no intention to render his position inferior to that of his colleagues or to prevent his acting in any other capacity than as a colonial secretary. The emphasis later placed upon the preamble definitely overlooks the fact that his patent designated him "one of our principal Secretaries of State" and assigned to him all the privileges and emoluments of that office.

Strictly speaking, the term "American Department," as applied to the office of Third Secretary, was a misnomer. Hillsborough did take over that part of the work of the Southern Secretary which related to the colonies, but that included a vast assortment of colonial possessions. The term may have been elastic enough to include the thirteen American colonies, Canada, Nova Scotia, St. John's Island, Newfoundland, and the British West Indies, but it could scarcely include Senegambia and the coast of Guinea in Africa, which fell definitely within the scope of the department's activities.[10]

Since Hillsborough and his successor, the Earl of Dartmouth, were peers, there was no opportunity to raise the ghost of the Place Acts of Queen Anne in their case.[11] Nevertheless the impression existed that this was a new as well as an inferior office. The chief obstacle to the appointment of General Conway as Third Secretary in August, 1767, had been the opinion of the Attorney-General that he would be barred from taking his seat in the House of Commons.[12] Had Townshend accepted the post, he would have been raised to the peerage to avoid trouble. Even Newcastle had tacitly agreed that this would be a new office. Benjamin Franklin described the recently established Colonial Office to his son as "a new distinct department" formed by the appointment of "a Secretary of State for America."[13] *The Annual Register* referred to it in similar terms. When Lord George Germain, a commoner, was chosen to succeed Dartmouth in 1775, to avoid any embarrassing interpretations the tell-tale preamble was omitted from his patent.[14] In 1779, his supporters successfully defended his right to sit in the House of Commons on the basis of precedents which occurred subsequent to the Place Acts of Queen Anne. Sir Joseph Mawbey, who challenged that right, secured only one convert to his point of view.[15]

When Edmund Burke in 1780 introduced in the House of Commons his Bill for Economical Reform, he referred to the American Department as one "commonly called or known by the name of Third Secretary of State or Secretary of State for the Colonies." Lord George Germain promptly protested against the qualifying clause and maintained that his official position as "one of His Majesty's principal Secretaries of State" gave him exactly the same status as the other Secretaries.[16] The wording was changed accordingly to conform to his interpretation, but the Act of 22 George III, cap. 82, which formally abolished the Colonial Department, contained the original qualifying clause.[17] Germain's defense of the unity of the Secretariat was upheld in an able speech by William Pitt in the House of Commons in 1797 denying that the office of Secretary of State was subject to departmental division.[18] Their opinion rather than that of the critics of the third secretaryship eventually prevailed.

Whether or not he did have authority to perform the functions of his colleagues in domestic and foreign affairs, the fact remains that the American Secretary actually confined himself to colonial business. Thomas De Grey, Junior, one of Germain's Under-secretaries, declared in the House of Commons in 1779 that Lord George, in the absence of the other Secretaries, sometimes introduced foreign ambassadors. This was, however, the only instance he produced of his chief's assumption of the duties of the two "ancient" Secretaries.[19]

Toward the end of the session in which Hillsborough became Secretary, both the legality and the expediency of his appointment were questioned in a debate in the House of Lords. The substance of this debate, in Alexander Wedderburn's hand, is preserved among the Newcastle Manuscripts in the British Museum.[20] Those who defended the appointment seem to have cited the usual precedents in its favor, but as Wedderburn was not primarily interested in this side of the case, his report dealt chiefly with the objections. The arguments of the opposition on the ground of legality were definitely weak. They contended that there could be only one Secretariat, and that by usage its functions could not be exercised by more than two. In support of this they cited the Regency Acts of 1751 and 1765 which presupposed the existence of only two principal Secretaries. They applied the statute of Queen Anne's reign, which prohibited the appointment of any additional commissioners for the execution of any office, to the position of Third Secretary. Above all, the opposition doubted the propriety of creating a distinct American Department, thereby separating the Colonies still more from Great Britain. Their challenge of the expediency of the new arrangement probably reveals the real objections of the critics. They argued that the First Lord of Trade was the most improper person to act as Colonial Secretary, since with the Board of Trade to support him he would undoubtedly attempt to assume control of the administration and to override the Privy Council. Although this argument was quite in keeping with the general impression that Hillsborough was not a Secretary of State in the full meaning of the term, but merely "First Lord with seals and cabinet,"[21] it completely overlooks the fact that he was Colonial Secretary for six months before he became

President of the Board of Trade.[22] Wedderburn reports that this debate would have been renewed in the following session had not other matters distracted the attention of the House.

The American Department was soon accepted as a fact. But the initial tendency to disparage it as an "inferior" department may well have inspired sundry sporadic attempts to deprive it of power and patronage, of which more will be said in another chapter.[23] There seems to have been no basis in fact for this interpretation, other than the wishful thinking of the Secretaries of the Northern and Southern Departments, together with the above-mentioned preamble, which implied that the Third Secretary was to be a Colonial Secretary. It was the American Revolution rather than the fact that the American Secretary was President of the Board of Trade which actually brought about the realization of the fears of the opponents of the Colonial Department. It made of the Third Secretary not only "one of His Majesty's principal Secretaries," but in practice, at least until defeat loomed on the horizon, *the* principal Secretary of State.

---

1 Albert H. Smyth (ed.), *The Writings of Benjamin Franklin* (New York, 1905-07), V, 89, B. Franklin to Wm. Franklin, January 9, 1768.

2 *Massachusetts Historical Society Collections*, 5th Series (Boston, 1885), IX, 252, Wm. S. Johnson to Pitkin, December 26, 1767.

3 There is a copy in the British Museum. It was addressed to Hillsborough as "Secretary of State for the American Department." The price was 1/6. The author deplored the tendency of nominating military and naval officers to govern colonies, and lamented the little good poetical imaginations did at the Board of Trade. To avoid depopulating England and at the same time to populate the colonies, he proposed to export foreigners who took refuge in London, a project which he thought could be managed at a cost of £20 per man per annum. By the appointment of able governors who would encourage agriculture, particularly wheat farming, as well as the fishing industry and the fur trade, he believed that Canada might become "a very valuable jewel in the British Crown." He proposed the abolition of the monopoly in the Newfoundland fishery and the opening up of the East Indian trade.

4 *Ibid.*, p. 6.

5 See Thomson, *op. cit.*, pp. 1-2. The seals included the signet, the lesser seal, and the cachet. Once a Secretary received the seals, he could enter upon the duties of his office whether letters patent had been issued or not, and even

THE STATUS OF THE AMERICAN DEPARTMENT 31

if he had not yet taken the oath of office. As the cachet was used in sealing letters to sovereign princes, it would hardly be of use to the Colonial Secretaries, but it is impossible to say whether it was withheld from them on this account. Thomson says that the ordinary letters of the Secretary were sealed with his own private seal. See Shelburne Papers, Vol. 134, f. 131, "Account of Fees Paid by the Secretary of State on his Appointment," where it is stated that the Secretaries paid for the engraving of their own seals, although occasionally they charged this item to a contingent bill. The use of the seals in the Colonial Department remains something of a mystery. Anson in his *Law and Custom of the Constitution*, II, 169-70, describes their use in the early twentieth century as follows: "In the Colonial Office the signet is affixed to Commissions and also to Instructions; these last pass the sign manual but are not countersigned by the Secretary of State. The second seal is used for royal warrants and commissions countersigned by the Secretaries of State." Among the War Office papers there are a few letters from Germain, Knox, and Pownall in the Colonial Department with the seals attached. These would suggest that Germain used his own private seal in regular correspondence. Other letters show that Knox and Pownall used the same seal, although it differed from Germain's, which may indicate that there was a separate seal for the under-secretaries. See War Office Papers, W. O. 1, Vols. 681 and 682, for the years 1776 and 1777.

6 Brit. Mus., Harleian MSS, Vol. 2263, f. 338. Halifax said that a Privy Council Minute, recording the expediency of the appointment was the custom with respect to the Scottish Secretaries, but he may have been mistaken. See Brit. Mus., Add. MSS, 33030, ff. 295-96. Queen Anne in the case of Queensbury did speak of the change before the Council. See *Hist. MSS Comm., Mar & Kellie MSS* (London, 1904), p. 480, Mar to Grange, February 3, 1708-9. Mar was present at the Council.

7 Brit. Mus., Add. MSS, 33030, ff. 295-96. With respect to salary and other matters, Halifax thought that the Third Secretary should be placed upon the same basis as the other Secretaries.

8 P. R. O., Patent Rolls, 8 George III, pt. 2, memb. 9. *Cf.* with Weymouth's patent, 8 George III, pt. 2, memb. 10.

9 See for example, Dodington's *Diary*, p. 396, where Halifax is spoken of as " Secretary for the Plantations "; Brit. Mus., Add. MSS, 33030, f. 295, where Halifax discusses the manner of appointing "a Secretary of State for Plantation Affairs"; *ibid.*, 33001, ff. 225, 227, where Rockingham's plans contemplated the appointment of "a Third Secretary of State for America"; *Hist. MSS Comm., Dartmouth MSS*, III, 182, where Rockingham again refers to the office as " Secretary of State for the Colonies and Plantations "; Brit. Mus., Add MSS, 33001, f. 382, where Dartmouth was proposed as " Secretary of State for America"; Walpole in his *Memoirs*, III, 98, used the term " Secretary of State for America "; and in his *Letters*, VII, No. 1197, reported Hillsborough's appointment as " Secretary of State for America." An anonymous pamphlet discussed *The First Measures to be taken in the American Department* (London, 1768). After its establishment

the same terms were applied indiscriminately by the Secretaries themselves and by Governors and other colonial officials writing to them. Examples can be found in C. O. 217, Vol. 28, p. 299; C. O. 42, Vol. 36, p. 579; C. O. 5, Vol. 245, p. 59; Sackville MSS, America, 1775-77, No. 14, etc.

10 Gibraltar and Minorca, however, remained in charge of the Southern Department.

11 See chap. i, note 29.

12 Walpole, *Memoirs of George III*, III, 98-9.

13 Albert H. Smyth (ed.), *op. cit.*, V, 89, B. Franklin to Wm. Franklin, January 9, 1768.

14 P. R. O., Patent Rolls, 16 George III, pt. 2, memb. 4.

15 *Parliamentary History*, XX, 250 *et seq.*, March 11, 1779.

16 *Ibid.*, XXI, 194, March 8, 1780.

17 *Ibid.*, p. 194. See *Statutes at Large*, XIV, 262, for a copy of the act.

18 *Parliamentary History*, XXXIII, 976-77.

19 *Ibid.*, XX, 267.

20 Brit. Mus., Add. MSS, 34412, ff. 393-5. Wedderburn became Solicitor-General in 1771 and Attorney-General in 1778.

21 Knox Papers, X, 22.

22 See Basye, *op. cit.*, p. 179.

23 See chap. v.

# CHAPTER III

# ORGANIZATION AND PERSONNEL

The American Department acquired offices in Whitehall in the Treasury Building, near those of the Board of Trade and Plantations. The present Colonial Office seems to have no records or plans of the eighteenth century offices, and none have been located in the Public Record Office. However, records in the Board of Works Papers indicate that repairs were made in January, 1768, at the Cockpit, Whitehall, for an office for the Earl of Hillsborough.[1] It seems that the so-called "Montagu lodgings," or that part of them assigned to the Third Secretary, had been at the disposal of the Secretaries of State for at least fifteen years.[2] Thomas Hutchinson, former Governor of Massachusetts, later referred to the office occupied by John Pownall, one of the chief Under-secretaries of the American Department and Secretary of the Board of Trade, as the Duke of Monmouth's bedchamber.[3] It is unfortunate that a series of eight reports on the office presented to the House of Commons in May, 1780, by Mr. Under-secretary De Grey, cannot be located in the Parliamentary Papers, in the Treasury Papers, or in the Shelburne, Sackville, or Knox Manuscripts.[4] Although some of the material they contain is available elsewhere, the location of these papers would be of great value for a detailed study of departmental organization. They were not printed, and it is assumed that they were lost in the fire which destroyed the Houses of Parliament in 1834.

In the regulation of the new Colonial Office, the Third Secretary and his subordinates must have encountered many problems. Unfortunately, we know relatively little about how they dealt with them, or how they distributed the business among the various members of the staff. William Knox, one of the Under-secretaries, gave his colleague, John Pownall, the credit of having regulated the office so well at its first establishment that nothing more was necessary than to keep everything in the same order.[5] According to Richard Cumberland, Germain swept aside a great deal of red tape, putting an end to circumlocutory reports and inefficient forms which impeded business.[6] When Shelburne took over colonial affairs in 1782, he reported to the King that he found the American Department in "the most perfect order."[7] Whether he left it in the same state is another question. Knox accused him of ordering all the books and papers of the Board of Trade to be scattered "higgelty-piggelty" over the floor where they remained until his successor Townshend replaced them.[8]

The Colonial Department was organized on a basis essentially similar to the plan followed in the offices of the other two Secretaries. A survey of the Northern Department compiled in 1766 by William Burke, one of the Under-secretaries, shows that General Conway had a staff consisting of two Under-secretaries, a first clerk, two senior clerks, seven ordinary clerks, a chamber and deputy chamber keeper, and a necessary woman.[9] A somewhat similar procedure was followed in the American Department in 1768, where Hillsborough's staff included two Under-secretaries, John Pownall and Richard Phelps, one first clerk, William Pollock, two senior clerks, John Larpent, Junior, and Ambrose Serle, and at first only two ordinary clerks, William Sawer [or Sawyer] and John Hutchinson.[10] The number of ordinary clerks increased to four by 1770, to five by 1775, and from 1777 to 1782 there were six. Even during the American Revolution, when the responsibilities and correspondence of the Colonial Department increased enormously, its staff was never as large as those of the other Secretaries.[11] Strangely enough, the partition of the Southern Department did not effect any reduction in the number employed there. On the contrary, between 1768 and 1782 the number of clerks under the Southern Secretary ranged from eight to fourteen, but was usually ten. The Northern Department during the same period employed from eight to twelve clerks, but its staff was ordinarily limited to eight. William Pollock, the first clerk, was the only person transferred from the Southern to the Colonial Office in 1768, and when the Third Secretaryship was abolished in 1782, he found a place in the Home Office. Philip Muly and William Mitton filled the offices of chamber and deputy chamber keeper, and Elizabeth Muly, presumably the wife of the former, acted as necessary woman.

The appointment of a new Secretary of State does not seem to have entailed any change in the personnel of the office. In addition to Pollock, three of those appointed in 1768, John Larpent, Junior, William Sawer, and Elizabeth Muly were still serving when the department was abolished in 1782, and they received adequate compensation for their suppressed offices.[12] Occasionally members of the staff were transferred to other departments. John Lillingston Pownall, a clerk in the Colonial Office in 1770, was transferred to the Board of Trade by Hillsborough in 1772.[13] Ambrose Serle became Solicitor and Clerk of Reports for the same Board on the resignation of John Pownall in 1776.[14] In 1782, three clerks, the veteran William Pollock, Eardley Wilmot, and George Palman were absorbed into the staff of the Home Office.[15]

The Colonial Department affords a good illustration of the nepotism which was so chronic in Government offices in the eighteenth century. John Lillingston Pownall was a son of John Pownall, the senior Under-secretary in the American Office and Secretary of the Board of Trade until 1776. Another of his sons, the Honorable George Pownall, was Secretary and member of the Council of Quebec. His more famous brother, Thomas Pownall, a former Governor of Massachusetts, had also served in the Board of Trade. John Larpent's father was first clerk in the Southern Department, and Pollock's father was one of the King's messengers attending the Colonial Secretary in 1774. When Thomas De Grey, Junior, served as Under-secretary in the Colonial Office from 1778 to 1780, his father, Sir William De Grey, was one of the Lords of Trade.

Four persons, two peers followed by two commoners, acted as Secretary of State for the Colonies between January, 1768, and March, 1782.[16] The Earl of Hillsborough, the first occupant, was succeeded in August, 1772, by the Earl of Dartmouth. When the direction of hostilities against the American colonies rendered the position distasteful to Dartmouth, Lord George Germain relieved him of the office. Welbore Ellis, who served barely a month, from February to March, 1782, is scarcely entitled to special consideration as a Colonial Secretary. During the same period there were seven changes in the Northern and five in the Southern Department, although it must be borne in mind that Weymouth served twice and Rochford once in each of those offices. Hillsborough, who became head of the Southern Department in November, 1779, was the only member of the Colonial Office to receive an appointment as one of the "ancient" Secretaries. The heads of the Northern and Southern Departments were without exception peers and the two commoners in the Colonial Office eventually received titles. Lord George Germain became Viscount Sackville on the eve of his retirement in 1782, and Welbore Ellis terminated his career as veteran placeman in 1794 with the title of Baron Mendip. The fact that Germain and Ellis were members of the House of Commons was of great importance to the Prime Minister during the American Revolution, when questions on colonial issues were an almost daily occurrence in that House.

Seven Under-secretaries served the Colonial Department between 1768 and 1782: John Pownall, Richard Phelps, William Knox, Christian D'Oyley, Thomas De Grey, Junior, Benjamin Thompson, and John Fisher.[17] When the department was first organized Lords North and Grafton were in favor of appointing Benjamin Franklin as Under-secretary.[18] Franklin, himself, was not enthusiastic about the post, and he was right in assuming that he was "too much of an American" in outlook to be selected for it.

There were always two Under-secretaries employed in the Colonial Department at one time, and although there seems to have been no official distinction between them, in practice at least, one was informally recognized as Senior and the other as Junior Under-secretary. They were appointed by the Secretary of State rather than by the Crown and it was their duty to receive and supervise the execution of his orders. Perhaps fortunately for the department, their term of service was not affected by the political maneuvers incidental to the removal of a Secretary of State, as was often the case in the offices of the other Secretaries.[19] The incoming American Secretaries followed the precedent set by Dartmouth in reappointing the Under-secretaries of their predecessors, and exercised their prerogative of independent choice only when a vacancy occurred.[20] John Pownall remained in the department for eight years, from 1768 to 1776, and William Knox for twelve, from 1770 to 1782. In no case before the abolition of the department were any of the Under-secretaries dismissed.

It was not the practice of the Colonial Office to draw its Under-secretaries from the ranks of the clerks, although such a procedure was characteristic of the other departments.[21] The American Under-secretaries were recruited from the other administrative offices in England and the colonies, or they were newcomers in Government service. On the whole, they were not men who were ignorant of colonial conditions, although their understanding of them was not always commensurate with their experience. John Pownall had served since 1761 as Secretary of the Board of Trade, and Christian D'Oyley had been Deputy Secretary at War before entering the Colonial Office. Three of the Under-secretaries had lived in the American Colonies, and one of these, Benjamin Thompson, was a native of Massachusetts. The other two, William Knox and John Fisher, were selected from the colonial bureaucracy, Knox having been Provost Marshal of Georgia for five years and Fisher Collector of Customs at Salem, Massachusetts. All three can be classed as persecuted Loyalists, a circumstance which undoubtedly colored their outlook on colonial affairs.

Officially there were no Parliamentary Under-secretaries in the eighteenth century, although usually some of the Under-secretaries were members of the House of Commons.[22] John Pownall was the first of the American Under-secretaries to secure a seat in Parliament. In November, 1775, shortly after Dartmouth's resignation, he was elected member for the borough of St. Germains, Cornwall, and he retained his seat until May, 1776, when he left the Colonial Office to become Commissioner of Excise.[23] In 1776, when he entered the Colonial Department, D'Oyley was re-elected as member for Wareham, Dorsetshire. Thomas De Grey, Junior, was an active member of the Lower House from 1774 until he succeeded to the title of Baron Walsingham in 1780. William Knox, the other Senior Under-secretary, was never a member of Parliament.

The friendly and even intimate relations that often prevailed between the Under-secretaries and their superiors, well illustrated by the correspondence of Pownall with Dartmouth and that of Knox with Germain, gave them a very real influence not only in the routine business of the department but in the formulation of policies.[24] Benjamin Thompson was a protegé of Germain and an inmate of his household. Although they were paid a salary by the Crown beginning in January, 1770,[25] and passed from the service of one Secretary of State to another, the Under-secretaries were in some respects more like confidential private secretaries than civil servants.

There is no evidence to suggest that the distribution of business among the Under-secretaries and clerks in the Colonial Office was as carefully regulated as it was in the Treasury after 1776, where each member of the staff was assigned particular duties.[26] Shelburne had proposed such an arrangement for the Southern Department in 1766, but it was apparently ignored.[27] The Colonial Office seems to have followed the more haphazard arrangement characteristic of the offices of the other two Secretaries.[28]

The chief task of the Under-secretaries was the handling of the Colonial Office correspondence, a business which, owing to its importance, is dealt with in more detail elsewhere.[29] It will be sufficient to state here that the major responsibility rested with the senior incumbent of the office, and in the majority of cases even the routine correspondence left the office under his signature. There was a tendency to delegate a particular kind of work exclusively to one of the Under-secretaries, but there was no hard-and-fast rule. As one of the two was frequently absent from the office, the other had to be capable of doing the work of both. Pownall and, after his departure, Knox handled all the business concerning Indian presents.[30] D'Oyley, who was a particular friend of Sir William Howe and a former Deputy Secretary at War, conducted a large part of the military business after his appointment in May, 1776.[31] John Fisher took charge of the routine correspondence with the Board of Trade.[32]

There were certain miscellaneous duties that fell to the Under-secretaries in addition to their more regular employment. Pownall attended the King's levee in Dartmouth's absence, a procedure which, according to Lord Suffolk's instructions to his subordinate, William Eden, it was always proper for an Under-secretary to adopt on such occasions.[33] He also prepared memoranda of colonial business to be laid before the Cabinet,[34] and on one occasion, at least, no doubt as a result of directions from Lord North or Dartmouth, he issued the summons for a Cabinet meeting at Lord Rochford's office.[35] Early in 1775 Knox and Pownall were consulted on the preparation of the King's speech to Parliament, which anticipated the adoption of some conciliatory measures toward the Colonies.[36] On this occasion, Knox claims to have drafted the American clause with the assistance of Pownall.[37] Later, with the coöperation of Sir Grey Cooper, one of the Secretaries of the Treasury, he made some alterations in the Address of the

House in reply. By his own acknowledgment, however, this was the only case in which the Under-secretaries were so employed.

It was not unusual for Knox to prepare information for Lord George Germain for the defense of Government policy in the House of Commons. Early in 1778, when the Government was attacked in the House for employing Indians in the war against the American Colonies, Germain asked Knox to prepare an account of the orders issued by the department on that subject since he had assumed office.[38] In June, 1781, Knox produced arguments in support of the favorable disposition of the people of Georgia and the Carolinas to the British cause, claiming that their hesitation to take up arms was the result of intimidation, not disloyalty.[39] Even the other departments turned to him for assistance on like occasions. In December, 1778, he furnished information for Suffolk, the Southern Secretary, on the state of Dominica, for use in the House of Lords.[40] When the Committee of the House on Extraordinaries was attacking the provincial corps as a "great job" in 1780, John Robinson appealed to Knox to supply information for the defense of the expenses incurred for their equipment, since neither the War Department nor the Treasury knew anything about them.[41]

William Pollock was the chief clerk in the American Department during its entire existence.[42] He was the son of one of the King's messengers and began his career as clerk in the Northern Department in 1764. In 1767, Shelburne gave him a post in the Southern Office, where he seems to have been regarded as "a sober, diligent young man" who "minded his own business."[43] In 1768, he was transferred to the Colonial Department, where he had charge of the office papers and of making up the dispatches. In the latter business he was so extremely proficient that in twelve years he omitted only one enclosure—probably a record for methodical workmanship.[44] It seems that he also had charge of making up the accounts of the salaries and fees for the department, although the Colonial

Office Fee Book is not in his hand. The contents of one of his letters to Dartmouth [45] and two entries in the fee book itself, in the form of receipts, indicating that John Pownall and John Fisher received their fees and allowances as Under-secretaries from William Pollock, tend to corroborate this view.[46] In the rare instances when both Under-secretaries were absent he assumed charge of the arrangements with the Post Office for the dispatch of packet boats.[47] Pollock had a house in Downing Street not far from the Colonial Office. In 1782, when the American Department was abolished, Shelburne found a lucrative place for him in the Home Office where he remained until his death. After his death, his executrix, Hannah Pollock, presented three interesting manuscript volumes called " Secretaries' Precedent Books," stated to be the property of William Pollock, to Viscount Sidmouth, the Home Secretary.[48] They contain copies of documents illustrating many aspects of the activities of the department of Secretary of State, and may have applied to all three offices. It is not clear whether Pollock compiled them on his own initiative, or by instruction, or whether they were in use in the Colonial Department at all. The volumes are not in his handwriting.

In addition to the regular staff of the American Department there was usually a porter in attendance at the door, whose duty it was to turn away unwelcome visitors, and who was paid for such porterage as he undertook. Benjamin Franklin, during Hillsborough's régime, was more than once denied admission.[49] Perhaps Charles Buller's description of the unfortunate people who spent hours waiting for an interview in the office of Mr. Mother Country in the early nineteenth century may be applicable in part to the Colonial Department of the eighteenth century. Franklin complained that he usually had to wait three or four hours for an audience, and when, on one occasion, he was admitted promptly, he considered the event of sufficient importance to record it in his correspondence.[50]

The Colonial Office could also requisition the services of the King's messengers to carry important Government dispatches to the absent Secretary and to the packet boats, or to transmit messages to other officials in London or its vicinity.⁵¹ The appointment and management of the messengers attending the Departments of State were in 1766 transferred from the Lord Chamberlain to the principal Secretaries.⁵² In 1772, the Secretaries of the Northern and Southern Departments received permission to select sixteen of those best fitted for foreign service to wait upon their offices alone, to receive directions from them, and to be paid by their orders.⁵³ No doubt Rochford and Suffolk made the best of this opportunity, for a report of the remaining thirty-six messengers attending the Colonial Secretary and the King in 1774 makes strange reading.⁵⁴ Four of these attended the King only, ten others did not attend at all, and four more were due to be superannuated. One of the ten who failed to do any active service possessed extensive property, another was reported to be a man of very bad character, and still another served Lord Grantham, the British ambassador at Madrid. Not even an ample fortune and two sinecures, however, were sufficient to discourage William Dick from attendance. Under these circumstances, efficient service, even in time of emergency, was hardly to be expected from the twenty-two who did attend the Colonial Office. Germain on one occasion was sufficiently exasperated to ask that messengers who were too fat to ride over five miles per hour should take their places in the stage coach. Pownall proposed to deduct a month's pay from another for his tardy arrival at Dartmouth's home with important dispatches.

Nevertheless, the lot of the messengers could scarcely have been an enviable one. The position of those attached to the Colonial Office compared so unfavorably with that of the sixteen employed by the other departments that they outlined their grievances to Lord George Germain.⁵⁵ To obtain any compensation for their time, labor, and attendance at the office, they claimed that they had to charge suppositious journeys, which was done with the connivance of the Clerk of the Cheque from whom they received their pay. They had no allowance for

## ORGANIZATION AND PERSONNEL 43

horse hire or other expenses for short rides in or near London. Consequently when the King, Germain, or his Under-secretaries were in the country, they almost exhausted their meager funds. For inland journeys they received only sixpence a mile, with no allowance for tips for hostlers and post boys, and the Clerk of the Cheque deducted the several days consumed in that way from their attendance at the office. The messengers in the Colonial Department could attend only five months in the year, whereas their more fortunate colleagues in the other offices served constantly. Moreover, the other sixteen were paid every fortnight both for riding service and attendance, and they received in addition £25 a year for the upkeep of a horse. If any improvement was made in the condition of the messengers as a result of this petition, there is apparently no record of it. It seems justifiable to assume that in time of crisis the inefficient and inadequate messenger service may have been a contributory factor in the delay or defeat of important administrative projects.

The American Department would scarcely be classed today as a model of efficiency. Those who created it had no intention, however, of establishing a model department. They were not appalled by nepotism, the selection of a reactionary staff, the extension of the King's system, or an inefficient messenger service. In organizing and manning the new department they were governed by conditions already prevalent in other offices. The American Department compares favorably, both as regards organization and personnel, with the other departments of the British Government during the same period, and in particular with the other secretaryships.

---

1 Board of Works 4, Vol. 14, January 15, 1768.
2 See the London County Council's *Survey of London* (London, N. D.), XIV, 79.
3 P. O. Hutchinson (ed.), *The Diary and Letters of His Excellency Thomas Hutchinson* (London, 1883-6), I, 309.
4 *Journals of the House of Commons* (London, 1803), XXXVII, 858-59, May 18, 1780. Mr. Under-secretary De Grey presented to the House the following papers:

Account of the annual appointments of the Principal Secretary of State for the Department of the Colonies.

Account of the annual allowances from His Majesty to the two Under-secretaries of State in the Department of the Colonies which commenced in January, 1770.

Account of the patent offices granted to the Under-secretaries of State in the Department of the Colonies.

Account of Fees received in the Secretary of State's Office for the Department of the Colonies, 21 January, 1768, to 5 January, 1780, together with the distribution of them.

Account of Monies received at the Exchequer by John Pownall, or at the Treasurer of the Chamber's Office, in pursuance of letters written by the Secretary of State for the Colonies to the Lords of the Treasury and expenditure thereof for His Majesty's service.

Account of Bills for stationery, etc. delivered to the Secretary of State's Office for the Department of the Colonies from 21 January, 1768, to 5 January, 1780.

Account of Messengers' bills allowed by the Secretary of State for the Department of the Colonies from 21 January, 1768, to 1 January, 1780, distinguishing each year.

Account of Monies received by Mr. William Pollock, at the Treasurer of the Chamber's Office, or at the Exchequer, in pursuance of letters written at sundry times to the Lords Commissioners of His Majesty's Treasury and expenditure by the direction of the Secretary of State for the Colonies from 21st January, 1768, to 5 January, 1780.

These papers were evidently placed before the House in response to the order of the House of Commons of March 2, 1780. See *ibid.*, pp. 686-87. The order was transmitted by John Robinson to Knox on March 7, 1780, and at the same time he asked for duplicates to be filed with the Treasury Office. See C. O. 5, Vol. 152, p. 83. The duplicates, however, have apparently been removed from the Treasury Papers. The *Journals* state that all these accounts were preserved among the other papers of that session. They were not ordered to be printed and were probably burned in the fire of 1834.

5 William Knox, *Extra-Official State Papers* (2 vols., London, 1789), I, 28.
6 Richard Cumberland, *Memoirs* (Philadelphia, 1856), p. 201.
7 Knox, *op. cit.*, I, 26-7.
8 *Ibid.*
9 Shelburne MSS, Vol. 134, f. 129, "Annual Salaries of Clerks &c, in the Right Honourable Mr. Secretary Conway's Office"; there are other lists in the State Papers Domestic, Entry Books, Vol. 142, p. 1, Conway to the Earl of Bessborough and Lord Grantham, August 15, 1766; *Ibid.*, p. 39, there is a similar list for the office of the Northern Department on January 20, 1768.
10 Apparently the first complete list for the Colonial Department is in John Rivington, *The Court and City Register* (London, 1769), p. 288. Unfortunately, these records are not always accurate, and they are frequently incomplete. This one omits Richard Phelps as Under-secretary, although he

## ORGANIZATION AND PERSONNEL 45

was undoubtedly officiating. Joseph Haydn's *Book of Dignities* (London, 1894, 3d. ed.), includes him in 1768, although it fails to spell his name correctly. The official correspondence contains some of his letters.

11 See *The Court and City Register* for these years; Thomson, *op. cit.*, p. 129.

12 Treasury Papers, T 1, Vol. 579, No. 9, for a paper endorsed: "Schedule No. 2. The Office of Third Secretary of State, 1782"; also T 1, Vol. 338, p. 177, for a list of compensations granted for suppressed offices; there is another copy of the list of compensations in T 1., Vol. 594, pp. 100-101.

13 *The Court and City Register* (London, 1770), p. 116, lists J. L. Pownall as a clerk in the Colonial Office; that of 1771, p. 116, lists him in the Board of Trade. He was in fact appointed by Hillsborough to the latter office. See *infra*, p. 60.

14 Dartmouth MSS, No. 1654, Germain to Dartmouth, January 23, 1776. Serle went to America in 1776 and during his sojourn there he wrote many letters to Dartmouth on the deplorable conditions among the "rebels." See also, "Ambrose Serle, Secretary to Lord Howe, 1776-78," by Edward H. Tatum, Jr., in the *Huntington Library Quarterly*, II, 265-84 (April, 1938), which throws new light on Serle's activities in America.

15 Treasury Papers, T 1, Vol. 579, No. 9. "The Office of Third Secretary of State, 1782."

16 It is often difficult to determine the exact dates of the term of office of the Secretaries of State for the Colonies, owing to the fact that they frequently received the seals, took the oath of office and obtained their patents on different days. The Colonial Office Fee Book (State Papers Domestic, Various, Vol. 32) records the dates on which the Secretaries received and resigned the seals, except in the case of Hillsborough. This makes possible a more specific list as regards dates than that supplied by Thomson, *op. cit.*, p. 185.

Earl of Hillsborough received the seals, January 20, 1768, and took the oath of office, January 21; resigned, August 13, 1772.

Earl of Dartmouth received the seals, August 14, 1772, and took the oath of office the same day; resigned the seals, November 10, 1775.

Lord George Germain received the seals, November 10, 1775; resigned them, February 11, 1782.

Welbore Ellis received the seals, February 11, 1782; resigned them, March 27, 1782.

17 The following table of the dates of the term of office of the Under-secretaries has been compiled from many sources and made as specific as possible. The Colonial Office Fee Book in some cases helps to determine the dates.

John Pownall, January, 1768, to May, 1776. Pownall resigned as Secretary of the Board of Trade in January, 1776. On January 23, 1776, Germain informed Dartmouth of Pownall's withdrawal. See Dartmouth MSS, No. 1654. Pownall continued to serve as Under-secretary in the Colonial Department until May, during which time he continued to collect fees. On June 9, 1776, Germain informed Howe that D'Oyley had taken Pownall's place. See Sackville MSS, America, 1775-1777, No. 33.

Richard Phelps, January-February, 1768, to January, 1770. Phelps was Under-secretary in the Northern Department until February 16, 1768, and it seems likely that this date marks the beginning of his term in the Colonial Department, although he may have moved there before the formal transfer was completed. See Stowe MSS, Vol. 261, f. 123.

William Knox, January, 1770, to April, 1782. Knox remained for a short time with Shelburne after the fall of the North Administration.

Christian O'Oyley, May, 1776, to February, 1778. Thomas Hutchinson first heard of his appointment on May 17, 1776. Hutchinson's *Diary*, II, 55. He first reports his removal on February 7, 1778, and confirms it on the 10th. *Ibid.*, p. 184.

Thomas De Grey, Junior, February, 1778, to July or August, 1780.

Benjamin Thompson, July-August, 1780, to October 4, 1781.

John Fisher, October 5, 1781, to March or April, 1782. Shelburne told Knox that he did not intend to keep Fisher. See Knox Papers, X, 35.

18 Smyth, *The Writings of Benjamin Franklin*, V, 90, B. Franklin to Wm. Franklin, January 9, 1768; also *ibid.*, X, 244.

19 See Thomson, *op. cit.*, p. 130.

20 The Colonial Office Fee Book (State Papers Domestic, Various, Vol. 32) contains the following record: " His Lordship [the Earl of Dartmouth] has been pleased to appoint John Pownall and William Knox Esquires (late Undersecretaries to the Earl of Hillsborough) to be his Lordship's Undersecretaries." A certain Frederick Montagu offered his services to Dartmouth at this time. See Dartmouth MSS, Box 9, No. 378.

21 Thomson, *op. cit.*, pp. 130-31.

22 *Ibid.*, p. 133. By an order in council of August 21, 1841, one of the Under-Secretaries of the Foreign Office was designated " Permanent " and the other " Parliamentary."

23 *Parliamentary History*, XVIII, 9.

24 For further discussion of this point, see chap. ix.

25 See also *infra*, p. 50.

26 Chatham Papers, Vol. 231, " Treasury Department." There are two copies of this very valuable survey of the work of the Treasury. See also an interesting article, " The Office of Secretary to the Treasury," by D. M. Clark in the *American Historical Review*, XLII, 22-45 (October, 1936).

27 Shelburne MSS, Vol. 134, ff. 141 *et seq.*

28 See Treasury Papers, T. 1, Vol. 550, " List of the Secretaries of State's Offices of the Northern and Southern Departments."

29 See chap. viii.

30 See *infra*, pp. 56-7.

31 Knox Papers, X, 34. Knox says D'Oyley had the entire conduct of the military business, but the correspondence with the War Office contains some letters by Knox. See C. O. 5, Vol. 168, pp. 345, 381, 439, 455, 459, etc.

## ORGANIZATION AND PERSONNEL 47

32 C. O. 5, Vol. 250.

33 Brit. Mus., Add. MSS, 34 412, f. 188, Suffolk to Eden, February 9, 1772; Dartmouth MSS, No. 2178, Pownall to Dartmouth, September 23, 1772.

34 Dartmouth MSS, Box 12, No. 498 [1772], "Memorandum of business upon which the King's pleasure is to be taken."

35 *Ibid.*, Box 23, No. 1003, Sir Stanier Porten to Pownall, November 30, 1774. This is endorsed by Pownall: "In consequence of this note Mr. Pownall has summoned a Cabinet for tomorrow evening at Lord Rochford's office."

36 Knox Papers, X, 21, "Proceedings in relation to the American Colonies."

37 See *infra*, p. 139.

38 Knox Papers, IV, 10, Germain to Knox [undated, probably February-March, 1778]. Germain adds: "You have furnished me with answers sufficient for time past, but I wish to see what orders have been given by me since I have been in office."

39 *Ibid.*, IX, 30, June, 1781, endorsed by Knox, "Defence to be made in the House of Commons, 1781."

40 *Ibid.*, IV, 43, Germain to Knox, December 4, 1778.

41 *Ibid.*, V, 34, Robinson to Knox, April 21, 1780.

42 See Shelburne MSS, Vol. 134, pp. 123-25, "Account of Clerks in Shelburne's Office"; also C. M. Andrews, *Guide*, I, 58, footnote.

43 Shelburne MSS, Vol. 134, pp. 123-25.

44 Knox, *Extra-Official State Papers*, I, 28.

45 Dartmouth MSS, No. 1692, Pollock to Dartmouth, July 19, 1776.

46 State Papers Domestic, Various, Vol. 32, Colonial Office Fee Book.

47 For example, C. O. 5, Vol. 252, September 25, 1781, Pollock to Todd.

48 State Papers Domestic, Various, Vols. 7, 8, 9. The first covers the period, 1677-1725; the second, 1706-1780, the third, 1780-1810. The last two volumes are in the same hand, but it is not that of Pollock.

49 Smyth, *The Writings of Benjamin Franklin*, V, 300, Minutes of a Conference with Lord Hillsborough, January 16, 1771.

50 *Ibid.*

51 Dartmouth MSS, No. 1080, "The Office of Secretary of State, 1774."

52 State Papers Domestic, Entry Books, Vol. 141, p. 129, Richard Sutton to Philip Sharpe & Thomas Chetham, Clerks of the Checque, December 30, 1766.

53 State Papers Domestic, Various, Vol. 9, pp. 77-8 (Secretaries' Precedent Books, Vol. 2), Rochford and Suffolk to the Lord Chamberlain, May 6, 1772. There is a list of those chosen in State Papers Domestic, Entry Books, Vol. 141, p. 306.

54 Dartmouth MSS, No. 1080.

55 C. O. 5, Vol. 154, "Petition of the Messengers to Lord George Germain" [1776?].

## CHAPTER IV
## SALARIES, FEES AND EMOLUMENTS

THE creation of the American Department upset the distribution of salaries, fees, and emoluments which existed in the Northern and Southern Departments prior to 1768. The other two Secretaries were inclined to resent the appointment of a Colonial Secretary, who, in their opinion, had usurped a considerable portion of the profits and patronage which had hitherto accrued to them. Certain adjustments, therefore, had to be made, chief among which was the allotment by the Crown of a salary to each of the Under-secretaries in the three departments. It was logical that the principles which governed the financial arrangements of the two older departments in the matter of salaries and fees should be applied to the Colonial Office. To avoid trouble, every effort was made to place the three departments as much on a par financially as possible, but without much success. The finances and vested interests of the American Department, which were directly or indirectly disrupted by the Revolution, have been almost entirely neglected by historians in the past. Yet these factors were undoubtedly important in determining the attitude of the entire staff on colonial affairs.

Fortunately there is a complete schedule of salaries for the Colonial Department for 1774 when Dartmouth was Secretary, and another almost as adequate for 1782 during Germain's tenure of office.[1] The position of the American Secretary as regards salary was substantially the same as that of the Secretaries for the Northern and Southern Departments, although his income from the fees of office was usually less than theirs. Each of the three Secretaries of State received from the Crown a regular salary of £1850 per annum, which was augmented by an additional £3000 secret service money issued by the Exchequer,[2] £730 board wages paid by the Cofferer, and a patent salary of £100. The patent salary was paid at Christmas, but the rest came in quarterly installments. The

Secretaries also shared the profits of the *Gazette*, the official organ for the dissemination of Government propaganda, which in general totalled around £500.[3]

No Secretary was fortunate enough to receive the gross amount of his income from the above sources, for there was a material deduction from each part of it for fees or land tax. Dartmouth, for instance, in 1774 paid £797.14.0 in fees and land tax on his regular salary of £1850, £304.16.0 in fees on receipt of his secret service funds, another £86 for his board wages, and £13.16.0 out of his patent salary. His net income from these sources was therefore £4,477.14.0 instead of £5680. These figures are almost identical with the deductions made from the salaries of the other Secretaries about 1766.[4] Dartmouth's share of the fees of office amounted in 1774 to £623.13.4,[5] making his income for that year, exclusive of the profits of the *Gazette*, £5101.7.4. These figures coincide fairly well with the testimony of Thomas Hutchinson shortly after the appointment of Germain in 1775, to the effect that a Secretary of State's place was worth £5200 clear.[6] The Colonial Secretary did not receive the usual salary of £1000 granted to members of the Board of Trade, although he was its President from 1768 to 1779, during which time he was required to attend.[7]

The Third Secretary was entitled on assuming office to the usual one thousand ounces of white plate, provided he had not received the same in any other office of the Government in the same reign. The fees on Dartmouth's appointment amounted to about £150, and the engraving of the seals for use in his office to £50. As in all probability the distribution of these fees was in accordance with that of the Northern and Southern Departments in 1766, it is interesting to note that the Privy Council Office, the Sergeant Trumpeter, the Board of Green Cloth, the Attorney-General, the Signet Office, the Privy Seal Office, the Patent Office, the Treasury, the Auditor and Pells, and the Lord Chancellor's messenger all profited by the appointment of a Secretary of State in the eighteenth century.[8]

According to the same account, an incoming Secretary had to pay £13 for the clock and two books of maps, but this was refunded by his successor.

The annual expenses of the American Department were borne by the Secretary of State, the principal items being the salaries of the clerks, together with an allowance to the Undersecretary and first clerk whenever there was a deficiency in the fees of office. Dartmouth's expenses in 1774 amounted to £1187.14.3 of which £588.16.0 went to pay the salaries of the clerks, £398.18.3 to John Pownall and William Pollock to make up their fees, and £200 to cover the cost of coal, candles, and " sundry other articles." [9] This compares favorably with William Burke's account of the expenses of the Northern Department in 1766, which amounted to £1352.15.0.[10] It may be assumed, however, that the Colonial Secretary's expenses increased during the Revolution with the employment of additional clerks and the decrease in military fees after 1776. Germain seems to have spent over £1300 in 1781 for the upkeep of the American Office.[11] As in the case of the other departments, the Treasury paid the Stationer's bill for the Colonial Office. In 1781 this amounted to £1563.11.11.

Before 1770, it was customary for the Secretary of State to provide the salaries of his Under-secretaries from his own allowance. It has been erroneously assumed that this practice was continued throughout the eighteenth century. In July, 1770, owing to the diminution of fees in the Northern and Southern Departments after the establishment of the American Department, an annual allowance of £500 was granted by the Crown to each Under-secretary.[12] John Pownall was particularly fortunate. His salary of £700 for his offices in the Board of Trade was continued after he became Under-secretary, while he drew the regular allowance of £500 for his new post.[13] After June, 1768, he collected all the fees of Under-secretary, and if in any year they fell short of £452.11.0, the Secretary of State made good the deficiency.[14] He was the only person in the Colonial Office to hold these two positions and to draw

SALARIES, FEES AND EMOLUMENTS 51

the combined salaries. The others had to be content with a salary of £500. While Pownall remained in the office, Knox obtained an additional payment from the Secretary of State of £47.9.0, which was officially recorded as "the deficiency in his allowance."[15] This sum was apparently intended to reimburse him for the amount of fees due on his salary as Undersecretary. About the time of the departure of Pownall in 1776, the fees of Under-secretary were divided equally between the two incumbents of the office.[16] In April of that year a permanent arrangement fixed the fees of each at £250 per annum. As the fees themselves did not usually produce enough, the Secretary of State supplied the deficiency.

Part of the salaries of the clerks in the American Office was drawn from the fees of the Secretary of State.[17] Until 1765, the Under-secretaries and clerks in the other two departments enjoyed the right to frank letters and newspapers for transmission by the post.[18] George Grenville deprived them of a lucrative source of income when he discontinued this privilege as far as letters were concerned. In 1769, Parliament granted compensation to each of the three departments of state in the form of £500 per annum out of the revenue of the Post Office to be divided in varying amounts among the clerks.[19] Due to this arrangement, the first clerk, William Pollock, received a minimum allowance of £250 drawn entirely from the fees of office, together with an additional sum of £150 from the Post Office, making a total salary of at least £400.[20] The two senior clerks, John Larpent and Ambrose Serle, received £270 and £190 respectively, part of which came from the Post Office. The salaries of the ordinary clerks ranged from £80 to £135 annually. The chamber and deputy chamber keeper got £20.16.0 each, and the former increased his by a share of the fees of office.[21] Elizabeth Muly received £48, but the record implies that she was not permitted to make anything additional from the cinders.

The Colonial Office Fee Book, which is preserved in the Public Record Office, contains not only a complete record of the standard fees exacted for various appointments and services, but also of the distribution of the money received among the Secretary of State, the Under-secretaries, the first clerk, and the chamber keeper.[22] Every person receiving fees was required to post in an accessible place in the office an exact table of the amount due. The standard fee for everything the King signed, except instructions, was £6.7.6.[23] This sum was exacted for commissions in the army from the rank of Captain to that of Major General, for colonial appointments ranging from Provost Marshal and Secretary to Lieutenant-Governor, and for the commissions of the Superintendent of Indian Affairs and the King's Printer at New York. A license to sell trees, or to print a new map, a leave of absence, or the appointment of a Professor of Divinity in King's College, New York, involved the payment of the same fee. In each case £5 went to the Secretary of State, £1 to the Under-secretary, five shillings to the first clerk, and two shillings sixpence to the chamber keeper. The Governor of a colony paid £38.5.0 on his appointment for a warrant bill of three skins, three letters, and instructions. Out of this fee, £25 went to the Secretary of State, £9.10.0 to the Under-secretary, £2.15.0 to the first clerk, and £1 to the chamber keeper. The standard fee for everything signed by the Secretary of State, except stationers' and messengers' bills, was £2.2.6, of which £1.10.0 went to the Under-secretary, ten shillings to the first clerk, and half a crown to the chamber keeper. The reference of a petition to the Board of Trade from the American Department was included in this category. Nothing illustrates better the somewhat dubious eighteenth century practice of augmenting the salaries of under-paid public officials by fees levied on every type of service rendered. In this respect, the Colonial Office was merely following in the footsteps of the Northern and Southern Departments.

The Colonial Office fees never equalled those of the Northern and Southern Departments.[24] The offices of the two " ancient " Secretaries derived emoluments not only from military commissions in English, Scotch, and Irish regiments, but

SALARIES, FEES AND EMOLUMENTS 53

from the creation of peers, from ecclesiastical, diplomatic, and consular appointments, as well as from patents, pardons, and licenses issued for various purposes. The emoluments of the Colonial Department were derived only from colonial appointments and from military commissions of regiments serving in America.[25] Before the establishment of the Colonial Office, the fees collected in the Southern Department ordinarily exceeded those in the Northern Department, but after 1768 the position was reversed. This change was of little consequence, however, as the two departments pooled their fees and shared equally in the profits. The Colonial Department never participated in this coöperative enterprise, probably because of the mutual jealousy that existed between the old and new offices. The complaints of the Northern and Southern Secretaries about the reduction of their fees due to the appointment of the Third Secretary were hardly justified. The salaries paid to the Under-secretaries by the Crown after 1770 and the allowance from the Post Office more than compensated for any loss they may have experienced. Each office received £1000 from the King for the Under-secretaries and £500 from the Post Office, making a total of £3000. The Colonial Office fees never amounted to more than £2521.2.8.

During the fourteen years of its existence the Colonial Department collected £18,638.10.5 in fees.[26] In 1768, its comparatively modest income from this source totalled £882.1.3. Although there were occasional setbacks, the profits from fees tended to increase until they reached a maximum in 1776 with a total of £2521.2.8. The average fees received from 1776 to 1781 inclusive amounted to £1464.18.6 per annum. The noticeable increase in 1775 and 1776 was due to the large number of military commissions prepared in the Colonial Office after the outbreak of the American Revolution. Such evidence of prosperity on the part of the Colonial Department aroused jealousy in the other two offices.

There had never been any permanent understanding between the three offices over the distribution of military commissions, and consequently of the fees derived from them. Of course those of English, Scotch, and Irish regiments serving in the British Isles were invariably prepared in the older departments. When these regiments served in America, however, there was some foundation for a controversy over the preparation of their commissions. From the establishment of the Colonial Department some of the commissions for the officers of such regiments seem to have been made out there. When the commission was valid in America only, the same procedure was followed. Before the outbreak of the Revolution, however, none of the commissions of Generals were prepared in the Colonial Office, even in the case of Haldimand and Carleton who were serving in America.[27] The highest commissions prepared there during this period were those of Colonel and of Major General in America only. In 1770, when there was a promotion of general officers, none of the notifications were sent to Hillsborough's office. In 1772, however, when there was a promotion of Generals, Field Officers, and Captains, the notifications of Lieutenant Colonels, Majors, and Captains belonging to regiments serving in America were sent to the American Department, although none belonging to the Generals went there. Weymouth and Suffolk claimed that this " mistake " should not be regarded as a precedent.[28]

The outbreak of the American Revolutionary War threatened to deprive the Northern and Southern Departments of a lucrative source of income from the fees of military commissions. In 1775, the new commissions of Gage, Carleton, and Howe were prepared in the Colonial Office. In 1776, all the important commissions for Generals and Lieutenant Generals stationed in America, as well as those of Major Generals in America only, were prepared by the same department.[29] The fees of the Colonial Office in 1775 were nearly £900 more than in 1774, and in 1776 they were over £1400 in excess of the income of 1774. Weymouth and Suffolk laid the matter before the King, protesting that the notifications of 1772 were improperly issued, and contending that when a British rank was conferred by brevets, notifications could not with propriety be sent to the American Office even if the regiment were serving in America.[30]

As Germain anticipated, the " ancient " Secretaries won the battle, with the result that the Colonial Office fees dropped in 1777 to £887.10.0 and in 1778 to £836.5.0, figures that are comparable only to those of 1768, 1769, and 1772. Germain asked Knox and D'Oyley to figure out some method of retrieving their losses.[31] Apparently Germain himself came to the rescue, for there seems to have been no change in the system after 1777. The commissions of Major Generals in America only, and the appointments of Commanders in Chief in America and the West Indies continued to pass through the Colonial Department. There was some increase in fees during the next three years, but they never again reached the level of the years 1775 to 1776.

In addition to their income from salaries and fees, members of the American Department were permitted to hold sinecures. This custom, although profitable to the recipients, involved all the evils of absenteeism in colonial offices. Richard Phelps, and after him, John Pownall, held the lucrative post of Provost Marshal-General of the Leeward and Caribbee Islands.[32] Pownall received the office for his own life and that of his two sons, and William Knox estimated that it netted him £1000 per annum.[33] As Naval Officer for Jamaica, Pownall received an additional £450. During the Revolution, Benjamin Thompson became Secretary of Georgia. In 1781, William Pollock was appointed clerk of the Crown for Quebec and secured all the emoluments of his predecessor, Adam Gordon. Even William Dick, one of the Colonial Office messengers, was listed in 1774 as the holder of two sinecures. One of the clerks, John Larpent, held the appointment of deputy clerk in the office of the Lord Privy Seal.

William Knox retained his position as Provost Marshal of Georgia after he entered the Colonial Office in 1770, although in salary and fees it brought him only £160 annually.[34] Just why he was called upon to relinquish his post as Crown Agent for East Florida is not clear, for Richard Cumberland in the Board of Trade acted in the capacity of Agent for several Colonies, and in later years Adam Gordon, Under-secretary in the department for War and the Colonies, was Crown Agent for Lower Canada. In 1772, however, Knox received adequate compensation by his appointment as Secretary of New York in reversion to George Clark, who shortly after resigned his interest to Knox for the sum of £3000.[35] Knox farmed out this office to his deputy, Samuel Bayard, for a thousand guineas a year. During the two years prior to the outbreak of the Revolution, he [Knox] collected £800 from the secretaryship. One irate American who regarded such appointments as a public shame, thanked God in 1775 that Knox would not derive another farthing from the post.[36] He must have voiced the feelings of many of his compatriots when he wrote as follows: "To have those who have grown rich with our money by sinecures, places, pensions, and church living, be the very scoundrels who villify and abuse us most, is too much for flesh and blood to bear."[37]

Another lucrative source of income for two of the Under-secretaries, Pownall and Knox, was the management of Indian presents. Before the Revolution, the whole expense of the Indian Department, as regulated in 1765, was defrayed by the Commander in Chief in North America and placed to the account of military contingencies.[38] During the war, however, the Government's attempt to utilize the services of its Indian allies against the Americans necessitated some deviation from the established practice. The Treasury, therefore, adopted the policy of authorizing large consignments of Indian presents annually for the Colonies.[39] However, the Treasury did not attempt to select and ship the articles to North America. On receipt of information or directions from the American Secretary of the quantity needed, the Board delegated the task to an Under-secretary in the Colonial Office, who was in constant touch by correspondence with the Indian agents, and who received a commission of one and a half per cent of the cost of the consignment for his trouble.[40]

Between 1775 and 1779 goods worth £87,984.18.10 were sent to Quebec, Pensacola, St. Augustine, Georgia, and Nova Scotia.[41] In 1780, a supply amounting to £15,265.13.5 was sent to Quebec. In the following year another consignment totalling £38,743.7.5 went to the same destination, together with one of £7,721 to Georgia and South Carolina. In the spring of 1782 all previous records were surpassed when £63,861.17.7 were spent on presents for Niagara, Detroit, Montreal, and Michigan. Needless to say, the enormous sums devoted to the distribution of Indian presents failed to produce results commensurate with the expenditure involved.

After Pownall's departure from office in 1776, William Knox assumed the management of Indian presents. As a partial compensation for his American losses, he continued to execute this business until his retirement in 1782.[42] His profits, based upon the cost of the above consignments, were by no means inconsiderable. At a commission of one and a half per cent he must have collected approximately £1245 between 1776 and 1779, £692 in 1781, and £958 in 1782. In the last two cases, his income from Indian presents exceeded his salary as Under-secretary. Unfortunately, it was not until 1797 that the Commissioners on Fees and Gratuities wisely recommended that no official in the civil service should be permitted to execute any business for the public on commission, and their advice was accepted.[43] The failure of the Government to establish this rule at an earlier date may well have been responsible for the peculation which was said to be rife in so many departments during the Revolutionary War.

Under-secretaries could also act as Justices of the Peace after 1739.[44] John Pownall is said to have been Deputy Lieutenant for the County of Lincoln for many years, and in the Commissions of the Peace for the counties of Lincoln, Middlesex, Kent, Surrey, and for the city of Westminster.[45] In 1781 Knox was appointed to the Commission of the Peace for Middlesex.[46]

Under these circumstances the income of an Under-secretary must have been a comfortable one, although the others may not have fared as well as Pownall and Knox. Between 1770 and 1775 Pownall must have received well in excess of £2500 a year from fees and offices.[47] When he was appointed Commissioner of Excise in 1776, a pension of £600 a year was settled upon his wife, and he was permitted to retain his office in the West Indies.[48] Had the Revolution not intervened, Knox would certainly have obtained more than £1300 a year, entirely exclusive of the profits of his Georgia estates. In spite of his perpetual grumbling about the loss of his American offices and estates, the King's pension of £1200 a year, granted in 1778, which, according to Lord North, was considerably larger than any other pension given to an Under-secretary, enabled him to enjoy an income of at least £1950 a year from that date until 1782.[49] This figure does not include his commission on consignments of Indian presents which varied from year to year.

It seems apparent that the Colonial Department, like the Northern and Southern Departments, possessed a contingent fund from which small payments could be made without prior reference to the Treasury. At all events, the American Secretary, on his own initiative, sometimes authorized the expenditure of funds for special purposes and submitted the account to the Treasury for payment.[50] In 1776, Germain, whose humanitarian sentiments were the subject of frequent comment, directed Pownall to advance £177.7.4 to distressed Loyalists. On transmitting the account to the Treasury, he recommended that a further sum of £200 or £300 be issued to Pownall to defray similar expenses.[51] Some such arrangement may have been made, for the Colonial Office disbursed £63 among needy Loyalists in 1781, and an additional £102.10.0 for the expenses of four Savoyard priests who were being sent to Quebec.[52]

The control of colonial patronage, vested in the Southern Department in 1761, was transferred to the Secretary of the

American Department in 1768.[53] It is difficult to determine just how extensive this patronage was, since the Admiralty and Treasury had the right to make recommendations to some offices in the Colonies, more particularly those in the Navy and Customs Departments respectively. It seems to have been important enough, however, to warrant the efforts of the older departments to regain what they had lost in 1768. Among the Colonial Office Papers there is a list of places in the West Indies and North America which were at the disposal of the Secretary of State in 1748.[54] This differs considerably, however, from a similar list of offices to which the Board of Trade secured the right of nomination by virtue of the order-in-council in 1752,[55] and which were later restored to the Secretary of State. It would seem, therefore, that the control of colonial patronage was subject to some fluctuation.

John Pownall, who spoke with authority, regarded the post of Governor of Barbados as the most valuable and desirable office within Dartmouth's patronage, and he tried to obtain it for himself in 1772.[56] The position of Lieutenant-Governor of Antigua was a sinecure office in the patronage of the Colonial Secretary worth £300 per annum.[57] In 1772, Lord Rochford sought to acquire the patronage of the American Department in order that he might have at his disposal the two important offices of Clerk of the Courts in Jamaica and that of Secretary in Virginia.[58] On the eve of his appointment as Colonial Secretary, Dartmouth was warned by Frederick Montagu, an adherent of the Rockingham faction, to insist upon the whole patronage of his office, in particular the sole appointment of Governors.[59] The post of Naval Officer of New York, which might be expected to fall to the Admiralty, was definitely at the disposal of the American Secretary.[60] In 1782, the Surveyor of Lands and Forests in America was appointed by the Treasury, although in 1748 the nomination belonged to the Secretary of State.[61] Dartmouth appointed Knox as Secretary of New York and Germain gave Benjamin Thompson a similar appointment in Georgia during the latter years of the Revolution.

As presiding officer of the Board of Trade from 1768 to 1779, the American Secretary was entitled to nominate a clerk in that office to the first vacancy that occurred after his own appointment. Hillsborough selected John Lillingston Pownall in 1771, and Germain in 1779 nominated William Hughes.[62] In June, 1769, Hillsborough told Lord Charles Montagu that the Board of Trade had the right to recommend persons to supply vacancies in colonial Councils,[63] and he repeated this information in 1770 in a letter to Governor Wright of Georgia.[64] In 1780, however, John Robinson, Secretary of the Treasury, recommended a certain Mr. Bishop to William Knox as having applied to Germain for a seat on the Council of Barbados.[65] It is possible that when the Board of Trade was separated from the Colonial Department it may have lost its right to make nominations to colonial Councils. The subject of patronage is a complicated one and merits further investigation.

The whole financial setup in the American Department was characteristic of the eighteenth century. Although salaries were fixed, except in the case of certain minor officials, they were so augmented by fees, sinecures, and pensions that opportunities for enrichment and favoritism were many. John Pownall made his fortune out of his various appointments and Knox was rapidly following suit when the Revolution upset his plans for the future. It seems to have been an accepted principle that a member of the staff should use his position to secure additional emoluments, sometimes, unfortunately, at the expense of the Colonies he was expected to serve. Perhaps Edmund Burke was not altogether wrong when he told Parliament that the American Department was established in order to increase the power of the Crown by means of an exorbitant increase in the civil list.[66]

---

1 Dartmouth MSS, No. 1080, " Survey of the Office of Secretary of State, 1774"; Treasury Papers, T 1, Vol. 579, No. 9, Schedule 2, " The Office of Third Secretary of State, 1782."

2 Treasury Papers, T 1, Vol. 595, p. 217, "An Account of the Sums issued at the Exchequer for Secret Service money for 30 years preceding Christmas

# SALARIES, FEES AND EMOLUMENTS 61

last distinguishing the sums issued in each year and to whom issued," March 8, 1783.

3 Shelburne MSS, Vol. 134, p. 133, "The Office of Secretary of State" [1766].

4 *Ibid.*, p. 128, "Account of the Annual Allowances made by the Crown to a Secretary of State and the Nett Money he receives therefrom."

5 Compiled from the Colonial Office Fee Book, State Papers Domestic, Various, Vol. 32.

6 Hutchinson, *Diary*, I, 556, November 12, 1775.

7 C. O. 389, Vol. 39, p. 137, "An Account of the Total Expense and Charge of the Office of the Board of Trade for the last seven years preceding the 5 January, 1782, distinguishing each year." This shows that Dartmouth and Germain presided without salary.

8 Shelburne MSS, Vol. 134, f. 131, "Account of the Fees Paid by the Secretary of State on his Appointment."

9 Dartmouth MSS, No. 1080. The amount paid to Pownall and Pollock to make up their fees has been compiled from the Colonial Office Fee Book.

10 Shelburne MSS, Vol. 134, f. 132, "Yearly Expences of the Office of Secretary of State."

11 Office Expences, 1781.

| | |
|---|---|
| Clerks and Chamber keepers | £649.12.0 |
| Incidents | 344.10.5 |
| Under-secretaries to make up fees | 255.18.0 |
| First Clerk to make up fees | 132.10.0 |
| | £1382.10.5 |

See Treasury Papers, T 1, Vol. 579, No. 9, "The Office of Third Secretary of State"; also, Colonial Office Fee Book.

12 Treasury Papers, T 1, Vol. 550, "List of Secretaries of States' Offices of the Northern and Southern Departments." This document contains the following statement: "Undersecretaries of State in the Northern and Southern Departments, without any allowance from the Crown till 12 July, 1770, when in consequence of a very considerable diminution of their Fees, by the separation of the American Department, His Majesty was graciously pleased to make, and continue to each Under Secretary, for the time being, the allowance of £500 per annum." There is a rough draft of the same in State Papers Domestic, S. P. 37, Vol. 14, which contains correspondence with the Treasury about including the allowance of £500 in the report. Under-secretaries in the Colonial Department received a similar stipend in 1774. See Dartmouth MSS, No. 1080. In fact it must have been paid from January, 1770. See *Journals of the House of Commons*, XXXVII, 858, "Account of the annual allowances from His Majesty to the two Under-secretaries of State in the Department of the Colonies which commenced in January, 1770."

13 C. O. 389, Vol. 39, p. 135, "Account of the Total Expence of the Board of Trade." The net amount of the salary he received was £608.14.0. Pownall

paid a land tax and civil list duties out of his salary at the Board amounting to £91.6.0. Dartmouth MSS, No. 1080, states that he received £500 from the King.

14 Dartmouth MSS, No. 1080. The Colonial Office Fee Book shows that Richard Phelps received the fees from January until June, 1768.

15 Dartmouth MSS, No. 1080. Knox received £500 from the King. "The Fees upon the receipt of this sum, allowed to Mr. Knox out of the fees of Under-secretary of State." As the fees of Under-secretary did not usually suffice to cover Pownall's requirements, the Secretary of State had to supply the funds for Knox.

16 Colonial Office Fee Book. The first evidence of division is during the quarter from April 5 to July 5, 1776.

17 Dartmouth MSS, No. 1080.

18 State Papers Domestic, Various, Vol. 8, p. 173 (Secretaries' Precedent Book), E. Lewis to the Post Master-General, April 26, 1711. A marginal note states that this was the first instance of free postage for the clerks.

19 Treasury Papers, T 1, Vol. 550, "List of the Secretaries of States' Offices for the Northern and Southern Departments." The Colonial Office was receiving the same in 1774. Dartmouth MSS, No. 1080.

20 Dartmouth MSS, No. 1080. The following distribution was made among the clerks in 1774:

| Clerks | From Secretary of State | From Post Office | Total |
|---|---|---|---|
| William Pollock | £250 | £150 | £400 |
| John Larpent | 170 | 100 | 270 |
| Ambrose Serle | 120 | 70 | 190 |
| William Sawer | 80 | 55 | 135 |
| John Hutchinson | 60 | 45 | 105 |
| Charles Hanbury Williams | 50 | 40 | 90 |
| William Allen | 40 | 40 | 80 |
| Total | £770 | £500 | £1270 |

21 In 1774 the chamber keeper's fees amounted to £24. The average annual income of the chamber keeper from fees covering a period of fourteen years was about £34.

22 State Papers Domestic, Various, Vol. 32. In the Offices of the other Secretaries the same officials profited from fees. *Ibid.*, Vol. 31.

23 Brit. Mus., Stowe MSS, Vol. 163, ff. 168-9, "Table of Fees in the Secretary of State's Office." F. M. Greir Evans who prints this in his article on the "Emoluments of the Principal Secretaries of State in the 17th Century," in the *English Historical Review*, XXXV, 526-28 (October, 1920), says this document is in the hand of Dr. Andrew Coltrie Ducarel, who died in 1785. Ducarel was one of the Deputy Keepers of State Records.

24 See the Fee Books of the Northern and Southern Departments, State Papers Domestic, Various, Vols. 33, 34.

SALARIES, FEES AND EMOLUMENTS 63

25 For the dispute over Commissions by brevet see *infra*, pp. 54-5.

26 The following table of fees has been compiled from the Colonial Office Fee Book where only quarterly totals are available. It shows both the total annual income from fees and the distribution of them.

| Year | in £ Total | Secretary | Secretary Under- | Clerk | Keeper Chamber |
|---|---|---|---|---|---|
| 1768 ...... | 882.1.3 | 638.1.0 | 167.0.0 | 52.2.6 | 24.18.9 |
| 1769 ...... | 817.13.10 | 532.6.0 | 195.13.4 | 60.0.0 | 29.10.6 |
| 1770 ...... | 1366.17.0 | 856.0.0 | 368.10.0 | 110.0.0 | 31.7.0 |
| 1771 ...... | 1390.10.0 | 815.0.0 | 423.10.0 | 120.0.0 | 31.10.0 |
| 1772 ...... | 885.12.6 | 620.6.8 | 183.3.4 | 59.0.0 | 23.2.6 |
| 1773 ...... | 1013.4.6 | 586.13.4 | 315.16.8 | 89.5.0 | 21.9.6 |
| 1774 ...... | 1083.0.0 | 688.0.0 | 290.10.0 | 80.10.0 | 24.0.0 |
| 1775 ...... | 1976.5.0 | 1446.13.4 | 357.16.8 | 118.10.0 | 53.5.0 |
| 1776 ...... | 2521.2.8 | 1763.3.4 | 504.13.4 | 184.5.0 | 69.1.0 |
| 1777 ...... | 887.10.0 | 584.13.4 | 215.6.8 | 66.0.0 | 21.10.0 |
| 1778 ...... | 836.5.0 | 635.13.4 | 133.6.8 | 44.10.0 | 22.15.0 |
| 1779 ...... | 1033.13.6 | 687.6.8 | 239.6.0 | 79.0.0 | 28.1.0 |
| 1780 ...... | 1812.2.6 | 1320.0.0 | 317.10.0 | 120.5.0 | 54.7.6 |
| 1781 ...... | 1698.17.6 | 1195.0.0 | 339.0.0 | 117.10.0 | 47.7.6 |
| 1782 ...... | 433.15.0 | 323.13.4 | 70.6.8 | 26.10.0 | 13.5.0 |
| | £18,638.10.5 | 11,497.3.8 | 4121.9.4 | 1327.7.6 | 495.10.3 |

27 Colonial Office Fee Book. See State Papers Domestic, S. P. 41, Vol. 26, Lewis to Porten, September 22, 1777, transmitting a paper respecting the precedents relative to commissions by brevet.

28 *Ibid.*, Porten to Lewis, September 23, 1777.

29 The commissions for Howe and Carleton as generals, those for Clinton, Percy, Burgoyne, Cornwallis as lieut. generals, and those for Massey, Vaughan, Pigot, Jones, Grant, Philip, Prescot as major-generals in America only, were made out in the American Office. Later in the year Clinton became a general in America. See also C. O. 5, Vol. 168, p. 297, Barrington to Weymouth, May 2, 1776. Barrington notified him that he had sent to Germain's office the notifications of officers for the 3rd and 4th battalions of the Royal American Regiment, "Lord Barrington conceiving that the Commission of a corps, which can serve only in the colonies, must of course fall within the Department of the Secretary of State for America."

30 State Papers Domestic, S. P. 41, Vol. 26, Porten to Lewis, September 23, 1777.

31 Knox Papers, III, 43, Germain to Knox, September 26, 1777.

32 P. R. O., Patent Rolls, 8 Geo. III, pt. 4, memb. 12 for Phelps and 11 Geo. III pt. 5, memb. 14, for Pownall.

33 Audit Office Papers, A. O. 13, Vol. 36, Knox to Munro, February 28, 1788.

34 Knox Papers, I, 8, Knox to Lyttleton, February 10, 1762. To provide for his two sons he later resigned the office and it was granted to his father-

in-law, James Ford, during their lives. See Chatham Papers, Vol. 223, Petition of William Knox and James Ford to the House of Commons.

35 Patent Rolls, 12 Geo. III, pt. 4, memb. 5; Rodney Papers, Vol. 15, "Brief State of Mr. Knox's Case" (Printed); Chatham Papers, Vol. 223, Petition of William Knox and James Ford to the House of Commons.

36 M. W. Willard (ed.), *Letters on the American Revolution, 1774-1776* (Boston and New York, 1925), p. 184, Extract of a Letter by the packet by a Gentleman at New York, August 3, 1775.

37 *Ibid.*

38 C. O. 5, Vol. 146, Pownall to Robinson, December 15, 1775.

39 Knox Papers, X, 2, "Precis of Orders for sending Indian presents" (1775-1779).

40 C. O. 5, Vol. 251, Knox to Grey Cooper, April 27, 1779; Treasury Papers, T 1, Vol. 559, W. Knox's Observations on Extraordinaries for Indian presents, 1780.

41 Knox Papers, X, 2; *ibid.*, 12, Memorial of William Knox to the Treasury [1782]; Treasury Papers, T 1, Vol. 573, "Comptroller's report on account of goods provided by William Knox's commission, 11 July, 1782."

42 Haldimand Papers, B. 45, p. 86, Knox to Nepean, December 28, 1782: "I think it proper to mention that the Agency of purchasing Indian presents devolved to me from Mr. Pownall upon his quitting the Secretary of State's Office, and that I had reason to believe the Commission was continued to me in consideration of the great increase of important business, and diminution of profits the American War occasioned to the Under Secretary, all the emoluments arising out of the thirteen revolted provinces having ceased and the military appointments throughout the continent having been given up to the Commander-in-Chief."

43 *Reports from Committees of the House of Commons* (London, 1803-06), "Sixteenth Report from the Select Committee on Finance," p. 297.

44 State Papers Domestic, Various, Vol. 8, pp. 111-12, Newcastle to the Attorney-General, January 15, 1738/9, asking if this could be done, and the reply (p. 112) was favorable.

45 John Nichols, *Literary Anecdotes of the 18th Century* (London, 1812-16), VIII, 66.

46 Knox Papers, VI, 29, Duke of Northumberland to Knox, November 23, 1781.

47 From the Board of Trade, £700; from the salary of Under-secretary, £500; from the fees of Under-secretary, £452.11; as Provost Marshal, £1000; total, £2652.11.

48 Audit Office Papers, A. O. 13, Vol. 36, Knox to Munro, February 28, 1788.

49 Sackville MSS, Home Affairs, 1751-1784, North to Sackville [February 16, 1782].

50 C. O. 5, Vol. 149, Knox to Robinson, June 2, 1777; Treasury Minutes, T 29, Vol. 48, p. 26, December 17, 1778; C. O. 5, Vol. 147, p. 187, Pownall to Robinson, February 16, 1776; *ibid.*, Germain to Treasury, February 26, 1776.

## SALARIES, FEES AND EMOLUMENTS 65

51 C. O. 5, Vol. 147, Germain to the Treasury, February 26, 1776.
52 Treasury Papers, T 1, Vol. 579, No. 9, "The Office of Third Secretary of State."
53 Colonial patronage is a subject which merits a separate study. It is only possible here to produce a few examples.
54 C. O. 5, Vol. 5, pp. 270-72.
55 Chatham MSS, Vol. 95. The document was published by Basye, *op. cit.*, Appendix B.
56 Dartmouth MSS, No. 2026, Pownall to Dartmouth, October 15, 1772.
57 *Ibid.*, Box 10, No. 412, Pownall to Dartmouth, September 6, 1772.
58 Knox Papers, X, 19.
59 *Hist. MSS Comm., Dartmouth MSS*, II, 87, Montagu to [Dartmouth], August 10, 1772.
60 Dartmouth MSS (Canadian Archives), Vol. 1, pp. 80-1, Pownall to Dartmouth, August 12, 1773.
61 Treasury Papers, T 1, Vol. 570, Knox to Grey Cooper, March 1, 1782. A similar statement is made in C. O. 218, Vol. 25, p. 343, Ellis to Sir And. Hammond, No. 1, February 28, 1782. The Collectors of Quit Rents apparently received their appointments through the Treasury. See C. O. 218, Vol. 25, p. 202, Dartmouth to Legge, June 7, 1775.
62 On this subject see C. O. 5, Vol. 156, Pownall to De Grey, April 15, 1779; *ibid.*, De Grey to Pownall, April 16, 1779; *ibid.*, Pownall to ————, April 17, 1779; C. O. 391, Vol. 86, pp. 139-40, June 15, 1779, Board of Trade Minute.
63 C. O. 5, Vol. 392, Hillsborough to Montagu, June 7, 1769. See Basye, *op. cit.*, pp. 77-8, who says that the one office which remained constantly at the disposal of the Board was that of Provincial Councillor.
64 C. O. 5, Vol. 677, p. 45, Hillsborough to Wright, July 31, 1770.
65 *Ibid.*, Vol. 152, Robinson to Knox, June 3, 1780.
66 *Parliamentary History*, XXI, 56.

## CHAPTER V

## THE FEUD WITH THE "ANCIENT" SECRETARIES

THOMAS POWNALL'S ideal of an independent American Department with unlimited authority to deal with all colonial issues, and to direct the other departments in these matters, was hardly achieved by the establishment of the Third Secretaryship in 1768. During the years from 1768 to 1775, and to some extent even during the Revolution, the American Department had to be constantly alert and alive to the intrigues of the "ancient" Secretaries in the Northern and Southern Departments. No doubt encouraged by the initial battle over the status of the Third Secretary,[1] his two colleagues frequently plotted to reduce his prestige and to regain the patronage and emoluments of the Colonial Office. At times their machinations threatened the very existence of the American Department.

When Lord Hillsborough became Secretary of the newly established American Department in January, 1768, he was inclined to believe that his department would not survive longer than six months.[2] According to William Knox, the two "ancient" Secretaries, Weymouth and Suffolk, never accepted Hillsborough as their equal, but chose to regard him as a somewhat glorified First Lord of Trade.[3] In 1772, Rochford, Suffolk, and Gower conspired to get rid of him with the ultimate object of overthrowing the North administration.[4] Their more immediate aim seems to have involved the control of colonial patronage. Rochford, at this time Secretary for the Southern Department, had his eye on two important colonial appointments which were about to become vacant, those of Clerk of the Courts in Jamaica and Secretary of Virginia. He would gladly have destroyed the American Department in order to regain the patronage for his own office.[5]

A suitable opportunity presented itself when Hillsborough, as President of the Board of Trade, took a vigorous stand in opposition to the extension of settlement west of the Alleghanies. In pursuit of this policy, he induced the Board to make an adverse report on a petition supported by Benjamin Franklin, Rochford, and others for a grant of 20,000,000 acres of land on the Ohio.[6] The refusal of Hillsborough's colleagues to accept the report induced him to resign rather than to attempt to execute a project so distasteful to him. As Basye contends, he resigned on the defeat of his policy as First Lord of Trade and not as Secretary of State.[7]

When it was known that Hillsborough would resign, the post of Third Secretary was offered to Lord Weymouth, the friend and adherent of Gower. Weymouth refused it on the pretext that his commission would confine his activities to the colonies and that the American Secretary was not, therefore, a Secretary of State.[8] Had Lord Dartmouth followed Weymouth's example, in all probability the administration of the colonies would have undergone another change. John Pownall thought it quite possible that the powers and patronage of the Third Secretary would be assigned to the First Lord of Trade.[9] In view of Rochford's interest in securing the patronage for the Southern Department, this seems hardly likely. Dartmouth's acceptance of the post defeated the conspiracy against Lord North for the time being, and frustrated the designs of Rochford. Pownall warned Dartmouth that he would not find his situation a bed of roses, but that Hillsborough's tactics had extricated the Department from many of the difficulties it had encountered in the beginning.[10]

The chief source of controversy between the old and new departments was the claim of the Colonial Secretary of the right to give orders to the Admiralty and the War Office, particularly with respect to the transport of troops to and from the colonies. The directions usually issued by the office of the Secretary on such occasions were as follows: to the Admiralty, orders to provide transports for troops en route to the colonies, to supply provisions for them during the voyage, to receive the troops on board, and instructions to sail for a particular destination;[11] to the War Office, orders to prepare the troops for embarkation, and later for them to embark.[12] In its broader aspects, the controversy involved the control of the army and navy in America, the West Indies, and Africa, for the King employed his Colonial Secretary to convey his pleasure to an Admiral commanding the fleet in colonial waters, and to the Commander in Chief of the forces in North America.[13]

Before the establishment of the American Department, the Southern Secretary issued the necessary orders to the Admiralty and the War Office. Hillsborough immediately began to issue similar directions when the troops were intended for the colonies,[14] and he corresponded with General Gage, the Commander in Chief, with regard to their reception and distribution in America.[15] During the crisis with Spain over the Falkland Islands in 1770, the Southern Secretary first challenged the right of the American Department to intervene in foreign and military business arising in North America and the West Indies. Lord North admitted that in certain respects that business was awkwardly handled, but he strongly suspected that the Southern Department made a mountain out of a mole hill in order to regain the patronage and emoluments of the American Office.[16] The controversy impressed the King, however, who was probably the recipient of complaints from both sides.

When the American Department changed heads in August, 1772, an attempt was made to prevent the recurrence of "future jarrings between the different departments,"[17] by divesting the American Secretary of all control of military and naval affairs in North America. Suffolk submitted a memorandum to the King asking that the Commander of the Fleet in America and the West Indies should transfer his correspondence from the American to the Southern Department; that the Commander in Chief of the Forces and all the Governors in

## FEUD WITH THE "ANCIENT" SECRETARIES 69

America should correspond with the Southern Department on all matters of a political nature which might arise between them and any Governor or officer of a foreign power; and finally, that all military arrangements or operations affecting America should, in time of war, be under the sole direction of the Southern Department.[18]

Suffolk might as well have asked outright for the abolition of the Third Secretaryship. The King, however, emphatically approved of his recommendations, and directed Lord North to broach the matter to Dartmouth.[19] Dartmouth's reaction to this attempt to encroach on the affairs of his department is not recorded, but Lord North was not impressed with the necessity of the proposed alterations.[20] Since the Colonial Secretary continued to conduct the correspondence with the Admirals and Commanders in Chief in America, and to transmit information from the Governors to the Southern Secretary when they related to foreign affairs, it may be assumed that there was no serious effort to put Suffolk's scheme into practice.[21] If there had been, the conduct of the American Revolutionary War could never have been undertaken by the Colonial Department.

Suffolk's *modus vivendi* had no bearing upon the transport of the troops to and from the Colonies. Nevertheless, in May, 1772, before Hillsborough left the office, Rochford, without any communication to the American Department, gave all the orders to the Admiralty and War Office for the dispatch of the 6th Regiment at Plymouth to relieve the 32nd at St. Vincent.[22] During the absence of Dartmouth in September, John Pownall discovered that the regiment was on the point of embarking, and he at once assumed the role of champion of the American Department against this "unwarrantable encroachment" by the Southern Secretary.[23] The business of relieving the troops at St. Vincent had been so badly managed that he was able to assume the direction of alterations necessitated by the unsuccessful war of Governor Leyborne against the Caribs. Pownall's changes involved the giving of discretionary power to Leyborne to detain the 32nd Regiment until the arrival of the 6th, and the ordering of an adequate supply of camp equipage for the 6th Regiment to prepare it for active participation in the war.

Rochford immediately challenged his right to intervene, but Pownall produced his precedent to show that in 1769, when the 8th Regiment went to America to relieve the 15th, all the orders were issued by the American Secretary.[24] With the King's support, he won the battle against Rochford, but before the final settlement took place, the Southern Secretary left for a vacation in the country and Pownall had to wage the battle all over again with Lord Suffolk, the Northern Secretary, who assumed "a much higher tone" in the matter. In the end, Suffolk agreed to expedite the orders as Pownall prepared them, and on this occasion they clearly indicated that the Northern Secretary officiated "in the absence of Lord Dartmouth" and not by virtue of his own prerogative.[25]

This victory over the two "ancient" Secretaries, however, was inconclusive. Both Rochford and Dartmouth continued to give orders for the transport and relief of troops, a situation bound to create confusion and to increase tension.[26] In January, 1773, Pownall protested to Dartmouth about the irregularity and improper conduct of the other departments toward them.[27] Dartmouth, himself, was never a vigorous champion of the prestige of his office. In interdepartmental, as well as in colonial relations, he was the exponent of conciliation, and although he seems to have condoned the belligerent attitude of his Under-secretary, he refrained, as far as possible, from assuming any personal role in the conflict. In February, 1773, on the occasion of Dartmouth's issuing directions for the transport of troops from Ireland to America, Rochford and Suffolk renewed the controversy, and demanded the withdrawal of his orders.[28] The King once more intervened with instructions for a report on the precedents. Those produced by the American Department were declared imperfect, and the new regulations approved by the King took the form of a compromise which favored the pretensions of the Northern and Southern Departments.[29]

This compromise provided that in the case of troops sent to the colonies in Africa and America from Great Britain or Ireland, where relief was not the object, the Secretary at War should notify the three Secretaries of State of the regiments to be sent, desiring one of the "ancient" Secretaries to take the King's pleasure for all necessary orders for their transportation and embarkation, and the Secretary of State for the Colonies to do likewise for the corresponding orders to the Commander in Chief or Governor in America for their reception and accommodation there. When relief was the object, the Secretary at War should notify the three Secretaries of State of the regiments or corps to be sent as well as those to return, desiring the "ancient" Secretary to give directions respecting the transportation and embarkation of the troops sent from Great Britain or Ireland, and the Secretary of State for the Colonies to transmit the orders to the Commander in Chief or Governor in America for their reception and distribution on arrival, together with any necessary directions for the embarkation and transportation of the troops which were to return. Finally, in the case of troops returning to Great Britain or Ireland from the Colonies, where no relief was sent out, the American Department was to direct the transportation and embarkation of the troops in the colony, while the "ancient" Secretary took charge of their reception and distribution in Great Britain or Ireland on their return. This complicated arrangement could hardly claim to have introduced greater precision into the business of transporting troops to and from the colonies. In time of peace, from 1773 to 1775, it seems to have sufficed, but after the war began its terms were no longer respected.[30]

The compromise over the relief and transport of troops did not do much to relieve the tension between the old and the new departments, for the Southern Secretary continued to usurp as much of the business of both offices as possible. Pownall regarded Lord North's blindness or indolence in neglecting to combat the arts practiced to ruin and disgrace the

Colonial Department as "astonishing and unpardonable." In July, 1773, he complained to Knox that while Bamber Gascoigne was "Minister for America" at the Board of Trade, and Lord Suffolk at the Privy Council, there was nothing for Dartmouth's miserable department to do.[31] A few months later, however, he found the courage to protest against a letter from Suffolk signifying the King's displeasure over the policy of encouraging emigration to St. John's Island and thereby threatening Great Britain with further depopulation. Pownall conceived that it was "unusual for one Secretary of State to signify the King's pleasure to another Secretary of State."[32]

The outbreak of hostilities in 1775 left Pownall little opportunity to play truant, for he was immersed in "the plentiful crop of difficulties" which the Secretary of State's office afforded, and overwhelmed by innumerable applications to the Board of Trade for leave to export gunpowder and ammunition to every place that he had ever heard of.[33] On this occasion, at least, he seems to have asserted himself successfully on the subject of securing supplies for the army, and on taking measures to prevent the fitting out of American privateers. In the absence of Dartmouth he formulated his own rules for the exportation of military supplies to Africa and America. He refused to let Suffolk's department present an address from the city of Liverpool to the King on the subject of the American controversy.[34]

Nevertheless, Pownall could not wage a successful battle single-handed against those who still conspired to disgrace the American Department. He assured Dartmouth that his absence from the office was irreconcilable with "that situation in which from motives of duty and most affectionate attachment" he wished to see him.[35] Dartmouth's distaste for the uncongenial employment of directing military operations against America induced him to ignore Pownall's appeal, and he remained absent during the critical months of September and October, 1775. On October 10, Pownall lamented to Knox that since Dartmouth had abandoned the office, William Eden, Suffolk's

Under-secretary, knew more about American affairs than he.[36] Pownall could not decide whether the disgrace of the department was due to Lord North's personal dislike of him, or to "some strange fascination" in Lord Suffolk and his subordinate, William Eden.

That the Colonial Department should have cut such "a pitifull figure" during the early stages of hostilities against America is certainly significant. For nearly seven years the contest for supremacy had been waged by the two "ancient" Secretaries, first on one issue and then on another. These years were of vital importance for the preservation of the connection between Great Britain and her restless American subjects. While the Secretaries of State were quarrelling among themselves over matters of precedence and prerogative, there was no chance of their finding a statesmanlike solution of the imperial problem. The lack of a vigorous and decisive leadership from the Colonial Secretary or from the Prime Minister, which might have silenced the perpetual intrigue in the other offices, left the Government ill-prepared to deal with a hostile America.

When Lord George Germain succeeded Dartmouth in November, 1775, only the serious nature of the crisis with America prevented another verbal combat, this time over the alteration of the wording of his commission as Third Secretary.[37] To offset the possibility of his exclusion from the House of Commons where Lord North needed him badly, the tell-tale preamble, which had created a definite impression that this was a new office, had to be omitted, and Germain's commission was identical with that of Weymouth, the new Southern Secretary. The King removed all further impediments by having Weymouth and Germain take the oath of office at the same time.

During the preparation of Germain's patent in December, Suffolk's department became the center of a well-laid conspiracy in which William Eden and Wedderburn, the Solicitor-General, were deeply concerned.[38] Both were inclined to fear, that with the discarding of the preamble, the Third Secretaryship would become the most honorable one of the three and that its prestige would lead to the disgrace and humiliation of the two "ancient" Secretaries. As the wording of his commission no longer confined the activities of the Third Secretary to the Colonies, they sought another means of achieving the same end. Eden, probably at Suffolk's behest, prepared a "barrier treaty" which declared the heads of the Northern and Southern Departments to be the two principal Secretaries of State with exclusive supervision of all business other than colonial, and confining the Third Secretary, who was always to be considered separate from the other two, to colonial matters exclusively.[39]

Wedderburn, apparently piqued by the disposition of Suffolk towards him at this time, raised objections to a treaty "calculated to circumvent Lord George in every case where credit is to be filch'd from him, & to load him with all the *Burthens* that may by possibility prove disgraceful or destructive."[40] He threatened to advise Germain to resign the seals rather than to accept a proviso which had never been demanded in the case of his two predecessors. Eden, amazed and discouraged by Wedderburn's desertion of the principles he stood for in 1769 and 1772, decided to refrain from further meddling, unless by his Captain's orders, "whether the ship lost a mizen mast or only a hen-coop."[41] Rumors of Carleton's defeat and the probable loss of Montreal seem to have put an end for the time being to this bickering about the punctilios of office. Eden sought to convince Pownall of the necessity for some barrier treaty, and through him to influence Germain, but the futility of this approach is obvious.

The outbreak of the American Revolution and the more aggressive leadership of Lord George Germain soon put an end to any rigid adherence to the clumsy compromise of 1773. The American Department assumed the responsibility for issuing most of the orders to the War Office and the Admiralty for the transport of troops and stores to America.[42] In January, 1776, Germain and Pownall made the necessary arrangements with both departments for the relief of Carleton at Quebec.[43] Orders for the embarkation of troops in Ireland continued to pass through the Southern Department to the Lord Lieutenant of Ireland, but transports for them were obtained on the initiative of the American Department.[44] Suffolk's project of 1772, designed to insure the leadership of the Southern Secretary in time of war, did not materialize.

The prestige of the Colonial Department increased considerably during the Revolution, the business and correspondence passing through the office multiplied tremendously, and it no longer cut the same pitiful figure as in October, 1775. In the words of Temple Luttrell in the House of Commons, Germain, by virtue of his office, became "chief Minister for the civil war."[45] By 1778, William Knox was conducting the bulk of the correspondence with Irish officials regarding the proposed relaxation of Irish trade restrictions, thereby encroaching on the sphere of the Southern Department.[46] It must be borne in mind, however, that while the American Department was primarily responsible for the execution of measures for carrying on the war, the formulation of those measures and the decision for their adoption did not rest with that office alone. Germain sometimes found that proposals which emanated from him received scant consideration from his colleagues, and he occasionally resorted to the ruse of presenting them through Lord North instead.[47] He complained that he and his staff were not consulted about the appointment of Commissioners to treat with the Americans in 1778, and in the drafting of their Instructions.[48] Moreover, he was not always able to prevent the other Secretaries from encroaching on his own sphere of activities. In 1777, they deprived his office of the emoluments received from fees for military commissions,[49] and in 1779 he lost the Presidency of the Board of Trade.[50] Nevertheless, until defeat loomed upon the horizon, his difficulties arose more often from the inefficient management of the other departments than from any attempt on their part to deprive him of prestige and emoluments.

---

1 See chap. ii.
2 *Grenville Correspondence*, IV, 247, Whately to Grenville, January 1, 1768.
3 Knox Papers, X, 22.
4 *Ibid.*, 19, Lord Hillsborough's Resignation.
5 *Ibid.*
6 *Ibid.*
7 Basye, *op. cit.*, p. 186.
8 Knox Papers, X, 22.
9 *Ibid.*, I, 51, Pownall to Knox, August 1, 1772.
10 Dartmouth MSS, Box 9, No. 377, Pownall to Dartmouth, August 8, 1772.
11 Typical examples can be found in the following volumes:

Orders for transports, C. O. 5, Vol. 241, p. 50; *ibid.*, Vol. 254, pp. 3, 268; *ibid.*, Vol. 263, pp. 116, 183.

Orders to receive troops or stores on board, C. O. 5, Vol. 254, pp. 26, 65; *ibid.*, Vol. 255, p. 24; *ibid.*, Vol. 260, p. 1; *ibid.*, Vol. 263, p. 199.

Orders to sail, C. O. 5, Vol. 254, pp. 7, 10, 45, 80, 106, 170, 262; *ibid.*, Vol. 255, p. 27.

Orders for convoys, C. O. 5, Vol. 254, pp. 11, 18, 52, 225, 240.

Orders for victualling troops during the voyage, C. O. 5, Vol. 254, pp. 22, 24, 42, 122; *ibid.*, Vol. 255, p. 2.

Orders for passage for officials going to America, C. O. 5, Vol. 254, pp. 58, 108, 198, 210, 283.

12 For orders to prepare the troops to embark, C. O. 5, Vol. 168, pp. 9, 85. For orders to embark, C. O. 5, Vol. 168, pp. 157, 233, 455, 459; *ibid.*, Vol. 169, p. 25.

13 For correspondence with the Commander in Chief, see C. O. 5, Vol. 174; *ibid.*, Vols. 233-240; *ibid.*, Vol. 263. The Colonial Secretary frequently conveyed the King's commands to the Admirals through the agency of the Lords of the Admiralty. For instance, C. O. 5, Vol. 263, pp. 24, 25, 37, 38, 92, 99.

14 C. O. 5, Vol. 241, Hillsborough to the Lords of the Admiralty, February 12, 1768; *ibid.*, Hillsborough to Barrington, February 12, 1768; *ibid.*, Hillsborough to the Secretary at War, February 20, 1768; *ibid.*, Hillsborough to the Lords of the Admiralty, July 28, 1768; *ibid.*, Hillsborough to Gage, July 30, 1768. See also Admiralty In-Letters, Vol. 4127, covering the period January, 1766, to November, 1769. After his appointment, January 21, 1768, Hillsborough gave all the orders for transports included in this volume.

15 C. O. 5, Vol. 241, Hillsborough to Gage, July 30, 1768. C. O. 5, Vol. 87 contains the correspondence of Hillsborough and Gage in 1769. There is no evidence of the participation of the other Secretaries.

16 J. B. Fortescue (ed.), *Correspondence of George III* (London, 1927-8), II, No. 1115, pp. 379-80, North to [Dartmouth], August 10 [1772].

# FEUD WITH THE "ANCIENT" SECRETARIES

17 *Ibid.*, II, No. 1110, p. 376, King to North, August 4, 1772; *ibid.*, No. 1113, p. 378, King to North, August 9, 1772. The King did not wish to disturb the patronage and emoluments of the Third Secretary.

18 *Ibid.*, II, No. 1112, p. 377, Suffolk to the King [August 7, 1772].

19 *Ibid.*, II, No. 1113, p. 378, King to North, August 9, 1772; see Dartmouth MSS, Box 9, No. 381, August 13, 1772, for the revised copy Dartmouth received.

20 *Correspondence of George III*, II, 379-80, North to [Dartmouth], August 10 [1772].

21 Thomson, *op. cit.*, p. 85, assumes that Dartmouth agreed, but if so the official correspondence gives no indication of it.

22 Dartmouth MSS, No. 2178, Pownall to Dartmouth, September 23, 1772; also Knox Papers, I, 56, Pownall to Knox, October 3, 1772.

23 Knox Papers, I, 56, Pownall to Knox, October 3, 1772.

24 Dartmouth MSS, Box 10, No. 429, Pownall to Dartmouth, October 8, 1772; see also *ibid.*, No. 430, Memorandum relative to the business in connection with the relief of troops going to or returning from America. This states that when Hillsborough assumed the Seals he found that Barrington had notified Shelburne that the 8th Regiment was to relieve the 15th at Quebec. Hillsborough, conceiving that the execution of all orders regarding troops going to or coming from America belonged to his department, gave directions for the troops to prepare to embark and for them to embark. Shelburne had already sent orders to the Admiralty.

25 *Ibid.*, Box 10, No. 429, Pownall to Dartmouth, October 8, 1772.

26 Admiralty In-Letters, Vol. 4129. Most of the orders came from the American Secretary. Letter 45 is from Rochford. See letters 80-81.

27 Dartmouth MSS, Box 13, No. 520, Pownall to Dartmouth, January 4, 1773.

28 *Ibid.*, Box 14, No. 558, Memorandum on the Relief of Regiments, February 11, 1763 [should be 1773] in Lord Dartmouth's hand.

29 *Ibid.*, Box 14, No. 573, February, 1773, Arrangement proposed concerning the transportation of troops from Great Britain or Ireland to the colonies in Africa and America, and as to their return from the colonies. Another copy in State Papers Domestic, S. P. 41, Vol. 26.

30 Admiralty In-Letters for this period; see *infra*, pp. 74-5.

31 Knox Papers, II, 2, Pownall to Knox, July 23, 1773.

32 Dartmouth MSS, No. 904, Pownall to Dartmouth, November 6, 1773.

33 *Ibid.*, No. 1500, Pownall to Dartmouth, September 7, 1775.

34 *Ibid.*, No. 1517, Pownall to Dartmouth, September 13, 1775.

35 *Ibid.*

36 Knox Papers, II, 32, Pownall to Knox, October 10, 1775.

37 The qualifying clause was omitted, P. R. O., Patent Rolls, 16 Geo. III, pt. 2, memb. 4. Knox Papers, X, 22, tells the story of how Germain became Secretary. The patent of Welbore Ellis was the same as that of Germain.

38 Brit. Mus., Add. MSS 34412, f. 392 [December, 1775]. In Eden's hand.

39 *Ibid.*

40 *Ibid.*, f. 398, Wedderburn to Eden, December 17, 1775.

41 *Ibid.*, f. 391, Eden to Wedderburn, December 16 [1775].

42 At first the other Secretaries issued some orders for transport. See P. R. O. Admiralty In-Letters, Vol. 4130, Nos. 164, 168.

43 C. O. 5, Vol. 254, p. 11, Germain to the Lords of the Admiralty, January, 1776; *ibid.*, pp. 28, 31, 45, 51, 52. For the arrangements with the War Office, *ibid.*, Vol. 168, pp. 9, 169.

44 C. O. 5, Vol. 139, Germain to Weymouth, February 12, 1776, March 19, 1776, April 29, 1776; *ibid.*, Vol. 143, June 3, 1780, December 15, 1780; *ibid.*, Vol. 254, p. 30; *ibid.*, Vol. 259, p. 70. The naval entry book for the Southern Department, State Papers Domestic, Entry Books, Vol. 232, shows that the other Secretaries had little to do with war operations, except in the case of Gibraltar and Minorca. Weymouth officiated once in 1777 during the absence of Germain. See C. O. 5, Vol. 254, p. 134, Weymouth to the Lords of the Admiralty, April 3, 1777.

45 *Parliamentary History*, XX, 263.

46 See *infra*, p. 146.

47 Knox Papers, IV, 52, Germain to Knox, January 12, 1779.

48 Sackville MSS, Letters to General Irwin, 1761-1784, Germain to Irwin, February 3, 1778.

49 See chap. iv, pp. 53-5.

50 See *infra*, p. 82.

# CHAPTER VI
# RELATIONS WITH OTHER DEPARTMENTS

THE American Secretary acted as agent for the transmission of the King's commands on colonial issues to the other departments of Government, as well as to the Governors, military and naval commanders in America, the West Indies, and Africa. In accordance with the custom of the other Secretaries, he did this by one of two methods: a warrant under the royal sign manual countersigned by him, or more frequently, by a letter under his signature.[1] The office of a Secretary of State enjoyed a certain superiority over the other departments where no Secretary presided, particularly in time of war. William Knox explained these circumstances for the uninitiated as follows:

Every one who is at all acquainted with the constitution of this Government must know that all warlike preparations, every military operation, and every naval equipment must be directed by a Secretary of State. Neither the Admiralty, Treasury, Ordnance, nor Victualling Boards can move a step without the King's commands so signified.[2]

There were, as we know, three Secretaries of State, and in spite of the constitutional fiction of the unity of the Secretariat, in the absence of any specific barrier treaty defining the functions of each, friction could and did easily arise.[3] Even when harmony prevailed among the Secretaries as to the exercise of their prerogatives, the successful execution of the King's orders depended upon the efficiency of organization and degree of coöperation of the departments which received their instructions. It will be well to examine the method and nature of the relations of the American Department with the other prominent departments of the Government.

In December, 1767, Lord Clare informed William Knox that his situation as President of the Board of Trade was in no way affected by the recent arrangements made for the creation of a Colonial Office.[4] In reality, the Board now stood in the same relation to the American Department as it had formerly to the Southern Department, for Thomas Pownall's recommendations for the merging of the two offices had not been carried out. Hillsborough as Third Secretary became an ex officio member of the Board. John Pownall, as Secretary of the Board and Under-secretary in the Colonial Office, served two masters, a position which, under some circumstances, might have become well-nigh intolerable.

In July, 1768, however, owing to political considerations,[5] a material change occurred in the relation of the two departments. Lord Clare was suddenly and somewhat unceremoniously transferred to the Treasury of Ireland,[6] a new commission was issued, nominating seven instead of the usual eight paid members of the Board, and Hillsborough was ordered to attend regularly. From this time until 1779 the American Secretary was President of the Board of Trade. Only on one occasion was his right to act in that capacity questioned, and the protest proved ineffectual.[7]

The change, although damaging to the prestige of the Board, was undoubtedly in the interests of efficiency, for it secured a more satisfactory co-ordination of the work of three departments, the Board, the Privy Council, and the Colonial Office. A circular letter sent by Hillsborough in July, 1768, to all the Governors in America, informed them that they need no longer send duplicates of their letters to the Board, but should confine themselves to one channel of correspondence — the Secretary of State for the Colonies.[8] It was then possible for him personally to bring matters of colonial concern to the attention of the Board, and to present its report to the Privy Council. Halifax had sought to transform the Board of Trade into a department of state, but as Basye so well explains, " the lesser office in reality was absorbed in the larger, and entirely disappeared as a separate department until 1779." [9] The significance of this change was not realized by Hillsborough's colleagues, who, entirely disregarding the fact that he had been head of the Colonial Department for six months before he became President of the Board, chose to consider him as First Lord with seals and a seat in the Cabinet.[10] The fact that his Under-secretary, John Pownall, had been connected with the Board since 1741 probably helped to perpetuate the fiction.

It is not an easy matter to distinguish the work of Hillsborough and Pownall as Secretary of State and Under-Secretary from their activities as President and Secretary of the Board. In general, however, it may be said that in his former capacity Hillsborough conveyed the King's commands to the Board, notified it of colonial appointments, ordered the drafting of commissions and instructions, gave directions concerning the preparation of the colonial estimates, called for information and reports for the benefit of his own office or for the Privy Council, and sometimes presented their reports in person to the Council.[11] As President he attended the meetings of the Board and signed its letters and reports.

After July, 1768, the Board, on some occasions, still corresponded directly with colonial Governors with respect to petitions or acts of the colonial legislatures which had been submitted to them for consideration.[12] It did not have to depend on the American Department to act as intermediary in its correspondence with the Treasury.[13] The prestige of the Board during this period was not high, however, although Hillsborough considered the rejection of its report in opposition to the colonization of the American West sufficient reason for resigning his post as Secretary of State in 1772.[14] A. H. Basye says that in 1774 the Board reached its lowest level with respect to the number of meetings and the amount of business transacted.[15] Pownall found it no easy task to assemble the Lords of Trade for the consideration of the African boundary dispute with the Netherlands, a problem turned over to the Board by the Northern Department.[16] At the outbreak of the American Revolution the Board was inundated with petitions for licenses to export gunpowder to all parts of the world. In general, however, the conflict deprived it of the greater part of its business. Richard Cumberland, in his *Memoirs*, referred briefly to the American war as "a business out of my office to be concerned in."[17]

One important change occurred in the relations of the Board with the Colonial Department in January, 1776, when John Pownall retired from his position as Secretary and Clerk of Reports.[18] His successor at the Board, Richard Cumberland, did not become Under-secretary of State, and Ambrose Serle, a clerk in the Colonial Office, succeeded him as Clerk of Reports. Cumberland's position lacked the prestige of Pownall's, and it necessitated an increase in the routine correspondence between the two offices, which was handled almost entirely by the Under-secretaries.

Pownall's resignation proved to be the first step in breaking the link between the Board and the American Department. The next change occurred in 1779 when, for political considerations, the Board was separated from the Colonial Office.[19] The threatened disaffection of Gower, Weymouth, and Suffolk forced Lord North to sail with the wind to prevent his ship from capsizing. The price of political peace was the admission of Lord Carlisle, the son-in-law of Gower, and one of the Peace Commissioners in America, into the Government as President of the Board. No other method seemed "so proper and convenient" to Lord North as the separation of the Board from the American Department. He did not feel that the change would in any way diminish "the emolument, credit, power or dignity" of Germain's position.[20] The King, who had recently asserted that Germain was of no use in his department, readily acquiesced in this solution. He went so far as to assure his American Secretary that this step would place him "in every respect on the same line as the two 'ancient' Secretaries."[21]

Germain had always considered himself primarily as a Secretary of State, and had seemingly discounted the importance of his position as head of the Board, although he was diligent in his attendance. Basye reports that he missed only 17 out of

179 meetings in four years.[22] On one occasion in the House of Commons, he so far disregarded the facts as to assert that he was no more a member of the Board of Trade than the Archbishop of Canterbury, although he sometimes attended as First Lord.[23] In June, 1779, however, he was not slow to insist on his right of patronage as First Lord, in the appointment of a clerk to the first vacancy in the Board.[24] Nor did he relish the prospect of the loss of that office a few months later, although he reluctantly acquiesced in the change.[25]

The appointment of Carlisle was duly achieved, in spite of Germain's chagrin, in November, 1779. It scarcely proved to be a step in the direction of economy. Whereas Germain had received no salary as President of the Board, Carlisle obtained £2000, actually twice the regular salary of a Lord of Trade.[26] Neither did the separation of the two departments serve the purpose for which it was intended of winning the support of Gower and Weymouth, who resigned shortly after. Carlisle soon deserted the Board to become Lord Lieutenant of Ireland, but even then the Presidency did not revert to Germain.[27] The Colonial Secretary from this time on was released from his attendance at the Board, and colonial officials were once again burdened with the necessity of sending duplicates of their correspondence there. The restoration of its nominal independence did not contribute much to the prestige of the Board, which along with the Colonial Office, was marked out for abolition in Burke's Bill for Economical Reform in 1780.[28]

The Colonial Secretary did not deal directly with foreign affairs, which were divided between the Northern and Southern Departments. Therefore, a great deal of the correspondence between them and the American Department related to colonial issues which developed foreign complications.[29] Rumors of Dutch or French encroachment on territory claimed by the British on the Guinea coast or in Senegambia, alleged intrigue by French and Spanish officers among the Indian allies of Great Britain in North America, proof of illicit trade between French ports and the American colonies, might require a protest to the foreign power concerned which could only be made through the office of one or the other of the two "ancient" Secretaries.

Occasionally, the other Secretaries invited the coöperation of the Colonial Office in dealing with thorny problems. In the case of Dutch interference on the coast of Guinea in 1773, Suffolk submitted a draft of his instructions to Sir Joseph Yorke, the British representative at the Hague, to Dartmouth for alterations or suggestions, and accepted his recommendation that the Dutch appoint a commissary to treat with the British.[30] A great deal of the correspondence interchanged between 1768 and 1775 was concerned with illicit trade between the Colonies and foreign powers, which required the combined efforts of the Secretaries to break it. For instance, information received by the Northern Department in October, 1774, from Sir Joseph Yorke, of a Rhode Island vessel loading with firearms at the Hague, led to the following steps being taken. The Northern Department transmitted the intelligence to the Colonial Office. Suffolk then directed Sir Joseph Yorke by a messenger dispatched in a special packet boat to secure the detention of the ship and the relanding of her cargo. Pownall, in the absence of Dartmouth, corresponded with Eden, Suffolk's Undersecretary, and with Philip Stephens in the Admiralty, to send a sloop or cutter to Amsterdam with instructions similar to those sent to the Admiralty. He then called a meeting of the Privy Council for issuing an order to prohibit the export of gunpowder, arms, or ammunition without license.[31]

The *Gazette*, the official news organ of the Government, was under the control of the Secretaries of State, who divided the profits between them.[32] The American Department selected items of news for publication from the dispatches and intelligence received from America, and transmitted this information to the Southern Department.[33] The staff also distributed copies of the *Gazette* to friends and officials in the Colonies. With the outbreak of the American Revolution the American Secretary exercised a more rigid censorship over what was published. John Almon, in referring to Germain's "dexterous management" of the *Gazette,* accused him of suppressing bad news and exaggerating good.[34] The suppression of news in time of war, however, is to be expected, and in the American Revolution it was sometimes due to the instructions of the King, Lord North, or one of the other Secretaries.[35] Germain declared himself in favor of publishing as much as could be done with propriety.[36]

There seems to have been a great disparity between the number of letters dispatched from the Colonial Office to the other Secretaries and those received from them, quantity at least being in favor of the Northern and Southern Departments. Once the war began, however, the volume of correspondence increased enormously on both sides, although the bulk of it was then left to the Under-secretaries. Protests from foreign powers concerning seizure or damage done to their ships or property in the British Colonies were referred to the American Secretary for investigation and report.[37] A very large proportion of the correspondence between the departments related to the German mercenary troops enlisted in Hanover, Hesse-Cassel, Anspach, etc., for service in America. The negotiations with the German princes or their agents were carried on by the Northern Department, which forwarded intelligence to the American Secretary about the number and equipment of the troops, the terms of enlistment, and the date of their arrival.[38] From the time they reached England, however (unless they were to re-embark in Ireland), they were at the disposition of the American Department, which gave orders for their transportation to America.[39] Even their letters were addressed in the first instance to the American Office and were forwarded from there to Germany or America as the case might be.[40]

Germain rather than Barrington was the real Secretary at War during the American Revolution. Barrington might submit proposals for the conduct of military operations but he had no real authority in the direction of them.[41] The War

Office confined itself to the more technical aspects of military organization, like the preparation of the army estimates for the House of Commons, the arrangement of the mode of relief for the troops each year, and the provision of tents, camp equipage, and medicinal stores for the army.[42] The overlordship of the Colonial Office during the Revolution was sometimes resented by the War Office. Barrington complained that his department rarely received original " states " of the army from the Commander in Chief, and was therefore reduced to the expedient of making application to the American Secretary for copies. His request for the alteration of this mode of procedure was refused. The War Office was permitted to receive monthly returns as usual direct from America, but had to be content to obtain copies of the " Effective States " through the office of the Secretary of State.[43]

The Ordnance Board, under the Master General and Principal Officers of the Ordnance, also received its directions from the Secretaries of State, which, for all practical purposes, meant that as far as American and African colonial affairs were concerned it was directed by the American Secretary. All kinds of ordnance stores, arms, ammunition, bedding, fire-engines, clothing for the troops, etc., were provided by this department and shipped in vessels supplied by the Admiralty or in those hired by the Ordnance Department at the direction of the Secretary of State.[44] The usual practice with respect to ordnance stores was for the Secretary at War to notify the Colonial Secretary of the needs of the army, whereupon the Colonial Secretary in his turn gave directions to the Board to supply them. The Board acted in response to warrants under the royal sign manual, countersigned by the Secretary of State, or to orders-in-council.[45] The Admiralty could obtain ordnance stores without the aid of the Colonial Secretary, but the Board of Ordnance could obtain transports from the Admiralty only through the auspices of the American Department.

In addition to the management of ordnance stores, the Board also controlled the artillery service and engineers. It had at its disposal a fund for military contingencies out of which money was paid by the direction of the Secretary of State. It prepared plans and estimates for the erection of fortifications in the Colonies and supervised the execution of them. When the officers of the Ordnance or their subordinates exceeded their instructions and erected more elaborate defenses than they were authorized to do, as in the case of Newfoundland in 1773, they were severely censured by the American Secretary.[46] The Board was notoriously slow in the preparation of ordnance stores for the use of the troops abroad. During the course of the war, Knox on more than one occasion upbraided them for delaying the convoy.[47] Sometimes, however, the Secretary of State was equally careless about responding to the representations of the Board. Three years passed before Hillsborough replied to their report on the ruined condition of the fortifications of Placentia.[48]

During the Revolution the dispatch of Ordnance store ships to America in safety presented a serious problem for the American Department. Early in 1776, Germain gave directions that all store ships and transports of the Ordnance bound for America be properly manned and armed in accordance with the practice during the Seven Years' War, and that they accommodate as many recruits on board as possible.[49] When feasible, the store ships sailed with convoy supplied by the Admiralty, but often there was no convoy available when they were ready to leave. In 1775, the *Friendship*, laden with blankets for the troops at Boston, waited six weeks for convoy and was eventually armed and dispatched independently. This practice not infrequently led to their capture by American privateers which lay in wait for them.

In August, 1776, Amherst and Townshend of the Ordnance Board recommended that stores be sent in forty-gun ships as the only means of insuring their safety in case of attack or separation from the convoy.[50] This was not done, but at the end of August Germain issued explicit directions for the protection of Ordnance store ships, none of which were to be employed unless provided with twelve carriage guns, each manned by three men.[51] Every ship was to receive two naval officers on board to direct her course, to accommodate as many recruits as possible, and to sail only with convoy. Germain asked the Board to notify the American Department regularly of the destination of each ship and of her accommodation for recruits. The entrance of France and Spain into the American War made it all the more necessary to insure the safety of the store ships. These regulations were ordinarily, but not rigorously adhered to, and some ships continued to sail without convoy, or with one instead of two naval officers, by special permission.[52]

Control over the Provincial Corps raised in America for service during the Revolution seems to have centered in the Colonial Department rather than with the Secretary at War.[53] The requisitions of clothing and accoutrements were prepared in the American Office and the goods forwarded to the Colonies by the Treasury. Benjamin Thompson and John Fisher had charge of the work in 1781. As in the case of Knox's management of Indian presents, there were many complaints about "jobbing" with respect to the arrangements for the Provincial Corps.

The Colonial Secretary assumed the direction of naval affairs in so far as this did not lie with the Admiralty. He, rather than the Lords of the Admiralty, conveyed the King's pleasure to the Commanders of the Fleet in America and the West Indies.[54] Frequently, however, the Colonial Secretary preferred to use the Admiralty Office as a channel for the communication of his directions to the Admirals.[55] Some of the more technical aspects of naval operations seem to have been left to the discretion of the Admiralty alone, for the Out-Letters of that office contain many orders which apparently did not originate in the American Department.[56]

The relations of the two departments were sometimes far from harmonious, and efficient coöperation was not always forthcoming. Germain perpetually complained of the "natural sloath of sea operations," which he came to regard as a necessary evil, and which he was sure he could not prevent.[57] Delay in the departure of Burgoyne for America in the spring of 1777 prompted him to ask Knox if two winds were necessary before the fleet could put to sea.[58] By the end of February, 1779, more than a month after Germain had ordered transports for reinforcements for Clinton, nothing had been done by the Admiralty and its subsidiary, the Navy Board, to secure them.[59] When the King became inquisitive about their preparations, Germain found that the Admiralty betrayed more expedition than usual in their own sphere.[60] Upon occasion the War Office joined with the Colonial Office in protesting against the unseaworthy ships supplied by the Navy Board for the transport of troops and stores.[61] There must have been faults on both sides, however, for the Admiralty on its part complained that it was not given adequate notice of the need for transports until it was too late to obtain satisfactory ones.[62]

The American Department came into touch with the Treasury in a great variety of cases where colonial and financial matters overlapped.[63] For instance, when Guy Johnson was appointed Superintendent of Indian Affairs, the Colonial Secretary transmitted a copy of his commission to the Lords of the Treasury in order that they might take the King's pleasure for annexing a salary to the office. This case is typical of the procedure followed with respect to other colonial appointments. Memorials for increase in salary, or for payment of compensation for extraordinary expenses, or for injuries received, seem to have found their way to both offices irrespective of which received them first.[64] In fact, the Treasury ordinarily refused to award financial compensation unless the petition were recommended by the Colonial Secretary.[65] During the war distressed Loyalists were supplied with funds in the same manner.[66] All problems related to the disposition or remission of quit rents, referred to the Colonial Secretary by the Governors, were turned over to the Lords of the Treasury for their decision.[67] The Treasury transmitted to the Colonial Department the orders of the House of Commons for the laying of correspondence or returns before them, and retained duplicates of documents so presented.[68]

Once the Revolution began there was a remarkable increase of correspondence between the two departments, chiefly relating to the victualling of the troops in the colonies, furnishing them with equipment, and supplying presents to insure the loyalty and coöperation of the Indian allies.[69] The Admiralty Victualling Board supplied provisions for the seamen and for troops in transit to America, but the Treasury entered into contracts with merchants for the victualling of troops during their service abroad. Similarly, the Treasury was called upon to furnish other necessaries for the conduct of the war not ordinarily supplied by the War Office or the Board of Ordnance. It made contracts for the sending of artificers to the Colonies. The actual business of providing Indian presents was delegated by the Treasury to one of the Under-secretaries in the Colonial Office, first to John Pownall and then to William Knox, who received a commission of one and a half per cent for their trouble.[70]

During the first part of the war the Treasury hired its own ships for the conveyance of victuals and equipment to America. When possible, the store ships sailed with convoy, and in any event, they received their complement of recruits and were armed in the same manner as the Ordnance vessels.[71] The dispatch of storeships to America by the Admiralty, Ordnance Board, and the Treasury did not contribute to unity of organization or efficiency. Independent action tended to increase the expense, and after France entered the war it became exceedingly dangerous to send armed victualling ships to America without convoy. In 1779, therefore, for motives of economy, security, and perhaps efficiency, the Lords of the Treasury made arrangements with the Navy Board to undertake the transport of their victuals and stores, and consequently discharged their own ships.[72] Germain, who was not consulted, and who was already familiar with the delays of the Navy Board in sending supplies to the seamen, expressed his entire disapprobation of the whole plan.[73] His protest proved unavailing, but Clinton's complaints about the scarcity of provisions soon gave him reason to point to the fulfilment of his prognostication.[74] In July, 1780, he protested to the Lords of the Treasury that in spite of their diligence in providing food, the delays of the convoys, together with the infrequency and irregularity with which they sailed, were prejudicial to the victualling service.[75] No doubt the Treasury was right in its refusal to return to the old system of independent action. More coöperation and efficiency on the part of the Admiralty were needed.

In addition to the points of contact already mentioned, the Colonial Department transmitted the King's commands and frequently other instructions to the Board of Customs Commissioners through the Treasury.[76] A direct correspondence between the Customs Board and the American Department was carried on by the Under-secretaries, relating chiefly to intercepted letters and to illicit or contraband trade.[77]

The Colonial Office dealt in much more deferential terms with the Treasury than with the War Office and the Board of Ordnance. At times, the Lords of the Treasury did act in response to the King's commands transmitted by the Colonial Secretary, but the supply of victuals and equipment for the troops and of presents for the Indians did not always call for an expression of the King's commands.[78] It was the practice of the Colonial Secretary or his subordinates, on receiving from the War Office information of the number of troops to be victualled during the current or forthcoming year, to transmit that information to the Lords of the Treasury, leaving them to take the proper action.[79] Pownall or Knox frequently notified John Robinson, the Secretary of the Treasury, of the rations or stores required, and asked him " to move the Lords of the Treasury " to supply them.[80] In some instances, Treasury orders were the result of consultation between the members of the two departments. To facilitate the dispatch of business and to co-ordinate the work of the two offices, one of the

Under-secretaries of the Colonial Department was sometimes summoned to attend the meetings of the Treasury Board.[81]

When there was a difference of opinion, as happened in April, 1780, over the quantity of provisions to be sent to Haldimand, the Treasury did not act contrary to the confirmed opinion of the American Secretary.[82] Occasionally, misunderstandings arose as a result of conflicting directions dispatched to colonial Governors by the two departments. For instance, the Treasury agreed in 1777 to permit the inhabitants of Bermuda and the Leeward Islands to purchase supplies from the Government stores.[83] Knox was present at the meeting of the Treasury Board when this step was determined. Unfortunately, the Colonial Secretary directed the Governors to permit the purchase of stores at prime cost, that is without charging for the freight, and the Treasury did not. Knox reminded Robinson that the Board had changed what he understood to be their purpose when he attended the meeting, and that the mistake would not have occurred had the Treasury transmitted copies of their letters to the Governors instead of the Treasury Minutes. Knox was in general on very good terms with Robinson, a fact which may have facilitated the dispatch of business between the two departments.

The Colonial Office was brought into close touch with the Post Office in matters relating to the packet boats which carried the Government dispatches as well as the regular mail to North America and the West Indies.[84] Shortly after the establishment of the American Department in 1768, Hillsborough, the former Postmaster-General, and Knox secured a monthly packet service to the West Indies and the southern Colonies. At this time, five vessels were engaged for the West Indies service, four for the southern Colonies, and four for the New York station. In 1770, a fifth boat was added to the New York route and shortly after a sixth was supplied for the West Indies. These arrangements were intended to facilitate a regular monthly service between Great Britain and all parts of His Majesty's dominions in America.[85]

Before the Revolution began the packet boats sailed at

fairly regular intervals, but even during this period the Colonial Secretary, or his subordinate acting for him, gave orders for their dispatch or detention and sometimes determined the route by which they went. Hillsborough, in particular, frequently failed to have his dispatches ready for the regular sailing date of the packets, and the interdepartmental correspondence contains numerous letters from Pownall to the Secretary of the Post Office ordering their detention until further orders.[86] Sometimes this meant a delay of one day, sometimes of ten, or even of seventeen days.[87] Permission for Government officials or private individuals to take passage on the American packets, with or without the payment of the King's passage money, had to be obtained from the Colonial Department, which instructed the postal authorities accordingly.[88] The packet boats themselves frequently belonged to the Commanders, who provided victuals and other necessaries at their own expense in return for an annual allowance from the Post Office.

The packet service was neither as efficient nor as fast as could have been wished. Hillsborough complained that the packets which left Falmouth in June did not reach New York until August 20, and ordered an investigation.[89] The Governors sometimes contributed to the further disruption of the service by detaining the packets in North America. In 1771, the *Comet* was detained twenty-seven days at Jamaica and seventeen at Pensacola. The Postmaster-General then recommended that Hillsborough instruct the Governors to pay the commanders £2 for every day's delay in the sailing of the packets.[90] This was done,[91] but it apparently failed to produce the desired effect. In the following year the Postmaster was still complaining of the almost constant detention of the packets by the Governors of Jamaica, South Carolina, and New York.[92] In 1775, he protested that the *Diligence* was detained by Governor Chester from September 25 to October 9 merely because the other packet was at Pensacola.[93] This was a hardship for the Commanders who were paid by the voyage, as well as a handicap to the service in general.

In September, 1775, John Pownall, acting under the instructions of Lord North, gave orders to the Post Office to discontinue the regular packet service to America.[94] During the Revolution, the packets were employed occasionally as the King's service required, and were dispatched according to directions received from the American Department.[95] They were armed for defense against privateers and their commanders instructed to sink the dispatches in case of capture.[96] Whenever it was possible Government dispatches were entrusted to warships convoying troops to America.[97] On several occasions the American Secretary gave instructions for the improvement of the service.[98] In 1778, Germain asked that the dispatches be forwarded in an oilskin bag to prevent damage from exposure to the weather. In September of the same year, during an investigation into the state of the packets, he directed that they be sheathed with copper and made more seaworthy.

The packet service during the war was the subject of much criticism owing either to delay in their dispatch from England or from America. In May, 1778, Germain complained to Clinton and Howe that none of the last five packets sent to North America had returned and that their frequent detention threatened to prevent any regular correspondence. They were warned not to detain one packet after the arrival of another, except in unusual circumstances.[99] In 1779, Germain asked the Post Office to notify the American Department of every day's delay in the departure of the packet boats after the mail had been received.[100] Clinton, too, often complained of the irregularity of the service. The reports of the Commissioners on Fees and Gratuities revealed the source of the expense, and of a least part of the mismanagement of the service, as due to the ownership of many of the packets by officers of the Post Office who were more intent on profits than on efficiency.[101]

The Colonial Secretary was himself a member of the Privy Council, and could, therefore, give personal attention to matters of colonial interest that came before that body. The correspondence that passed between the two offices was of a purely routine nature handled by the Under-secretaries.[102] It consisted almost entirely of the transmission of petitions and papers on colonial problems for the information and consideration of the Council in accordance with the King's wishes.

From this survey of the contacts of the American Department with the other branches of the Government, it can be seen that the Secretary of State for the Colonies played an important and decisive role, particularly during the Revolution. The American Department was the pivot upon which the entire organization of resistance to colonial independence turned. Unfortunately, the survey also reveals a marked lack of coöperation between the various departments of Government, especially in all matters pertaining to transportation of troops, food, equipment, and mail. Part of this was due to decentralization of control in the matter of transport. Some of it was probably due to ill feeling between the heads of departments, which usually spread to the Under-secretaries. Perhaps in these days, when speed of communications has become so commonplace, we may be inclined to exaggerate the injurious effects of the failure to expedite business which was so chronic in many eighteenth century departments and which even extended to the internal messenger service. It seems to have been one factor, however, and an important one, which contributed to the failure of Great Britain in the American War of Independence.

---

1 Thomson, *op. cit.*, p. 65.

2 Knox, *Extra-Official State Papers*, I, 14.

3 For the duel with the "ancient" Secretaries, see chap. v.

4 Knox Papers, I, 24, Viscount Clare to Knox, December 24, 1767. See A. H. Basye, *The Lords Commissioners of Trade and Plantations*, chap. iv, for the relations of these departments.

5 Walpole, *Memoirs of George III*, III, 225-6. The death of Cooke, one of the members for Middlesex, and the resignation of the younger Thomas Townshend from the post of Paymaster of the Forces, which he had shared with Cooke, seems to have caused the political rearrangement.

6 Smyth, *Franklin*, V, 148, B. Franklin to Joseph Galloway, July 2, 1768.

7 See C. O. 391, Vol. 86, pp. 139-40, June 15, 1779, Board of Trade Minute.

8 C. O. 5, Vol. 241, Hillsborough to all the Governors in America, July 4, 1768.

9 Basye, *op. cit.*, p. 179.

10 Knox Papers, X, 22, Secretaries of State.

11 C. O. 5, Vols. 154, 241, 251, contain typical examples of the type of correspondence that passed between the Colonial Department and the Board of Trade. See Basye, *op. cit.*, pp. 180-81.

12 C. O. 218, Vol. 7, p. 461, Lords of Trade to Francis Legge, February 27, 1776; *ibid.*, p. 474, Cumberland to Arbuthnot, June 22, 1776; *ibid.*, p. 493, Lords of Trade to Arbuthnot, March 18, 1777; *ibid.*, p. 494, Lords of Trade to Arbuthnot, June 12, 1777.

13 For example, *ibid.*, p. 497, Cumberland to John Robinson, August 8, 1777.

14 Knox Papers, X, 19, August 15, 1772, Lord Hillsborough's Resignation.

15 Basye, *op. cit.*, p. 190.

16 Dartmouth MSS, No. 898, Pownall to Dartmouth, October 20, 1773. Pownall said the Dutch were ready to open the conference but the Board of Trade wasn't. "Lord Robert Spencer begs to be excused, Mr. Jenyns can't come, Mr. Elliot certainly won't and Mr. Joliffe has sent no answer."

17 Cumberland, *Memoirs*, p. 195.

18 See *infra*, p. 101.

19 See A. H. Basye, "The Earl of Carlisle and the Board of Trade, 1779," in the *American Historical Review*, XXII, 334-39 (January, 1917).

20 Sackville MSS, America, Miscellaneous, 1774-1782, North to Germain, September 10, 1779.

21 Geo. Donne (ed.), *Correspondence of George III with Lord North*, II, 283.

22 A. H. Basye, "The Secretary of State for the Colonies," *American Historical Review*, XXVIII, 16 n. (October, 1922).

23 *Parliamentary History*, XX, 263, 266.

24 C. O. 391, Vol. 86, pp. 139-40, Minute of the Board of Trade.

25 Sackville MSS, America, 1779, Germain to North, September 13, 1779.

26 C. O. 389, Vol. 39, p. 137, "An Account of the Total Expence and Charge of the Office of the Board of Trade for the last seven years preceding the 5th of January, 1782, distinguishing each year."

27 Basye, "The Earl of Carlisle and the Board of Trade, 1779," *American Historical Review*, XXII, 339.

28 *Parliamentary History*, XXI, 235 *et seq.*

29 C. O. 5, Vols. 138-144, 241, and 247 contain many examples.

30 C. O. 5, Vol. 247, p. 141, Suffolk to Dartmouth, May 7, 1773; *ibid.*, Eden to Pownall, May 14, 1773; *ibid.*, p. 149, Suffolk to Dartmouth, July 27, 1773.

31 Dartmouth MSS, Box 23, No. 984, Account of steps taken upon intelligence rec'd from Sir J. Yorke of a vessel loading at Amsterdam with firearms.

32 Thomson, *op. cit.*, p. 148. See Treasury Papers, T 1, Vol. 550, "Secretaries of State's Offices, Northern and Southern Departments," where it is said that the writer of the *Gazette* was appointed by the King without any salary from His Majesty. As Thomson says, the office had become a sinecure.

33 For examples, see Knox Papers, II, Nos. 42, 43; III, Nos. 4, 31, 32, 51; VI, No. 26.

34 John Almon, *Biographical, Literary and Political Anecdotes* (London, 1797), III, 278 *et seq.*

## RELATIONS WITH OTHER DEPARTMENTS 97

35 For instance, see Knox Papers, III, 4.
36 *Ibid.*, 32, Germain to Knox, August 22, 1777.
37 See C. O. 5, Vols. 140-42 for examples.
38 *Ibid.*, Vols. 140, 141, 142, and 144 contain numerous examples.
39 C. O. 5, Vol. 254, pp. 51, 65, 221, 225, 238; *ibid.*, Vol. 255, p. 24; *ibid.*, Vol. 260, p. 1.
40 C. O. 5, Vol. 142, pp. 205-07, De Grey to Fraser, February 2, 1779.
41 Dartmouth MSS, Box 24, No. 1035, Barrington to Dartmouth, December 24, 1774. See the volumes of military correspondence, C. O. 5, Vols. 235-240, 243-4, 263, which plainly indicate that the important instructions on military operations emanated from the Colonial Department.
42 C. O. 5, Vols. 168-74. See Edward E. Curtis, *The Organization of the British Army in the American Revolution* (New Haven, 1926), chapter ii, for a more detailed account of the duties of the Secretary at War.
43 C. O. 5, Vol. 171, pp. 97-8, Lewis to De Grey, April 20, 1779; *ibid.*, De Grey to Lewis, pp. 183-4, November 13, 1779.
44 Typical examples of the correspondence of the Ordnance Office with the Colonial Department can be found in C. O. 5, Vols. 161-66.
45 The King's warrant was required before arms were issued. See C. O. 5, Vol. 162, Boddington to Knox, June 8, 1776.
46 C. O. 5, Vol. 161, Dartmouth to the Lieutenant General and Principal Officers of the Ordnance, February 20, 1773.
47 Examples in C. O. 5, Vols. 162, 163, 165.
48 *Ibid.*, Vol. 247, Lieutenant General and Principal Officers of the Ordnance to Hillsborough, February 25, 1772, p. 46.
49 *Ibid.*, Vol. 162, Pownall to Boddington, January 25, 1776; *ibid.*, Pownall to Boddington, February 9, 1776.
50 *Ibid.*, Amherst to Germain, August 15, 1776; *ibid.*, Townshend to Germain, August 21, 1776. The Admiralty turned this scheme down. See C. O. 5, Vol. 259, p. 99, Lords of Admiralty to Germain, August 28, 1776.
51 *Ibid.*, Vol. 162, pp. 597-600, Germain to Townshend, August 29, 1776.
52 For examples, C. O. 5, Vols. 162, 164.
53 Knox Papers, V, 34, John Robinson to Knox, April 21, 1780; see C. O. 5, Vol. 153, Germain to the Lords of the Treasury, October 12, 1781.
54 See C. O. 5, Vols. 243-44. In the case of the Vice-Admiral at Newfoundland, who was also its Governor, the Admiralty asked the American Secretary to provide any necessary alterations in his instructions. C. O. 5, Vol. 254, p. 40.
55 The best examples of this are in C. O. 5, Vol. 263, containing the secret correspondence.
56 Admiralty Out-Letters, Vols. 1332-40 (Secret Orders and Instructions), contain orders not issued by a Secretary.
57 Knox Papers, III, 13, Germain to Knox, June 15, 1777. See also, Curtis, *op. cit.*, chap. v, on "The Problem of Transportation."
58 Knox Papers, III, 9, Germain to Knox, April 2, 1777.
59 C. O. 5, Vol. 254, p. 254, Germain to the Lords of the Admiralty, February, 1779.

60 Knox Papers, III, 10, Germain to Knox, May 22, 1777.
61 C. O. 5, Vol. 259, p. 180.
62 *Ibid.*; also, Vol. 260, p. 86.
63 For relations with the Treasury, C. O. 5, Vols. 145-153.
64 C. O. 5, Vol. 145, Nos. 4, 5, &c.; *ibid.*, Vol. 247, pp. 47, 152.
65 The writer has found no instance of their granting compensation in defiance of the Colonial Department.
66 See C. O. 5, Vols. 147, 149.
67 For example, C. O. 5, Vol. 145, Pownall to Cooper, July 9, 1772.
68 See C. O. 5, Vol. 151, Grey Cooper to Knox, March 18, 1779, transmitting the Order of the House of Commons of February 15, 1779, and asking that the proper Return be made to the House and a duplicate be filed with the Treasury. See also C. O. 5, Vol. 152, p. 83, Robinson to Knox, March 7, 1780, transmitting the Order of the House of Commons of March 2, 1780. The Colonial Department was not always prompt in its response. In December, 1779, Robinson again asked for the Return called for in February, and in March, 1780, he was asking for a duplicate of the same.
69 See C. O. 5, Vols. 147-153, covering the years 1776-1781.
70 See *supra*, pp. 56-7.
71 C. O. 5, Vol. 147, Pownall to Robinson, February 5, 1776.
72 *Ibid.*, Vol. 151, Robinson to Knox, March 10, 1779; *ibid.*, Robinson to Knox, March 31, 1779.
73 *Ibid.*, Vol. 151, Germain to the Lords of the Treasury, March 16, 1779.
74 See, for example, C. O. 5, Vol. 100, p. 601, Clinton to Germain, October 31, 1780, where he reports that he faces the same melancholy prospect of being reduced to distress by want of provisions in spite of the repeated representations of the Commissary General. At this date he had not received one ounce of the year's supply, and Arbuthnot had sent the last consignment to Halifax without notifying him. On November 16, he reported the arrival of a provision fleet from Cork.
75 For this controversy, see C. O. 5, Vol. 152, pp. 359-62, Germain to the Lords of the Treasury, July 21, 1780; also the reply, *ibid.*, August 3, 1780; and Robinson to Knox, *ibid.*, pp. 501-08, September 22, 1780. The response of the Admiralty to Germain's representation of Clinton's complaints was that the victualling of the army did not depend on their office and they could give no directions concerning it. See C. O. 5, Vol. 260, p. 19, Lords of the Admiralty to Germain, December 13, 1780.
76 See C. O. 5, Vol. 146, where Customs material is included with the Treasury correspondence. See also E. E. Hoon, *The Organization of the English Customs System 1696-1786* (New York, 1938).
77 C. O. 5, Vols. 146, 148, and 149 contain typical examples of direct correspondence, all of which seems to have been handled by the Undersecretaries.
78 The Colonial Department frequently did transmit the King's commands to the Lords of the Treasury. See C. O. 5, Vol. 149, pp. 485, 497, 585, 627; *ibid.*, Vol. 150, pp. 533-34; *ibid.*, Vol. 152, pp. 9, 95-6, 381; *ibid.*, Vol. 251, p. 144.
79 *Ibid.*, Vol. 147, pp. 5, 15; *ibid.*, Vol. 150, p. 545.

## RELATIONS WITH OTHER DEPARTMENTS 99

80 *Ibid.*, Pownall to Robinson, February 14, 1776; *ibid.*, February 16, 1776.
81 *Ibid.*, Vol. 150, pp. 41-6, Knox to Robinson, January 16, 1778. Knox reports attending the Board on October 25, 1777.
82 *Ibid.*, Vol. 152, pp. 183-84, Robinson to Knox, April 24, 1780; and the reply, pp. 187-194, April 26, 1780.
83 *Ibid.*, Vol. 150, pp. 41-6, Knox to Robinson, January 16, 1778.
84 See C. O. 5, Vols. 247-49, In-Letters, Domestic, and Vols. 250-52, Out-Letters, Domestic.
85 Knox Papers, XI, 67, Knox to Lord Temple, November 2, 1782. Before this time the packets sailed only once in two months for the West Indies and Southern Colonies. See C. O. 5, Vol. 241, Hillsborough to Sandwich & Le Despencer, May 27, 1768. Hillsborough directed the change to be made with the consent of the Treasury, but Knox claims that it was due to his initiative.
86 *Ibid.*, for numerous examples.
87 For instance, *ibid.*, Pollock to Todd, April 21, 1768; *ibid.*, Pownall to Todd, July 9, 1768; *ibid.*, November 2 and November 19, 1768; *ibid.*, Pownall to Todd, May 3 and May 13, 1769.
88 C. O. 5, Vol. 251, p. 1, Pownall to Todd, March 27, 1776. This seems to have been a war measure.
89 *Ibid.*, Hillsborough to the Postmaster-General, October 12, 1768.
90 *Ibid.*, Vol. 247, Postmaster-General to Hillsborough, August 7, 1771.
91 Directions were sent by circular letter, C. O. 5, Vol. 241, but delays continued.
92 *Ibid.*, Vol. 247, p. 102.
93 *Ibid.*, p. 229.
94 Dartmouth MSS, No. 1558, Pownall to Dartmouth, October 7, 1775; the Governors were notified accordingly, C. O. 5, Vol. 242, October 5, 1775.
95 When South Carolina was restored to the King's peace in 1780, Germain ordered the restoration of a regular monthly service. C. O. 5, Vol. 252, June 28, 1780.
96 *Ibid.*, Vol. 251, Pownall to Todd, March 29, 1776, pp. 1-2.
97 *Ibid.*, pp. 163-4, Knox to Todd, May 9, 1778.
98 *Ibid.*, pp. 174, 181.
99 *Ibid.*, Vol. 243, Germain to Lord Viscount Howe and Sir Henry Clinton, May 4, 1778.
100 *Ibid.*, Vol. 251, p. 263.
101 *Reports from Committees of the House of Commons, 1715-1801*, XII, 179. Anthony Todd, the Secretary of the Post Office, was the owner of several packets.
102 C. O. 5, Vol. 133, Vols. 250-52. Orders-in-Council were made out "In obedience to Your Majesty's commands signified to us by the Right Honourable Lord George Germain, One of Your Majesty's Principal Secretaries of State &c." See C. O. 5, Vol. 32, January 24, 1781. Vols. 25-32 contain Orders-in-Council relating to the Colonies.

## CHAPTER VII
## BIOGRAPHICAL SKETCHES OF THE UNDER-SECRETARIES

THE Colonial Secretaries, Hillsborough, Dartmouth, Germain, and Ellis, are sufficiently well known to render any further analysis of their personalities and background unnecessary here. This is not the case, however, with respect to the seven Under-secretaries of the department, John Pownall, Richard Phelps, William Knox, Christian D'Oyley, Thomas De Grey, Junior, Benjamin Thompson, and John Fisher. Biographical information about the Under-secretaries is for the most part scarce, scattered, and sometimes unreliable. Only two of them, William Knox and Benjamin Thompson, have secured recognition in the *Dictionary of National Biography*. The rest must be traced in sundry memoirs and diaries, Loyalist records, and other widely separated contemporary sources. Since so little attention has been paid to them in the past, it has been deemed advisable, in view of the importance of their position in the department, to present the essential facts here in so far as they are available.

John Pownall (1725-1795), an elder brother of the well-known Thomas Pownall, was one of the two outstanding Under-secretaries of the Colonial Office.[1] He entered the Board of Trade in the humble capacity of clerk in 1741, and rose gradually to a position of prominence and responsibility. In 1745, he became Solicitor and Clerk of Reports for the Board. In 1753, he was appointed acting or joint Secretary and in 1758 he secured the Secretaryship, a post which was second only to the Presidency in importance. Finally, in 1768, at the age of forty-four, he united in his own person the offices of Secretary of the Board of Trade and Clerk of Reports for the same department with that of Under-secretary of State in the American Department.[2] Aside from his career as a bureaucrat, he was an antiquarian of some note and a Fellow of the society of that name. He had made a special study of the Roman archeological remains at Lincoln.

Pownall's political principles were in general those of Hillsborough and the North administration. A well-meaning friend of Dartmouth warned him anonymously in 1772 against his two Secretaries, Knox and Pownall, " who carry with them into office all the injurious and illiberal ideas and enmities public and personal of their late Lord." [3] Dartmouth does not seem to have heeded the warning, for he was a close personal friend of Pownall during his entire term of office. Under both Dartmouth and Hillsborough, Pownall exerted every effort to uphold the dignity and prerogatives of the American Department. His organizing ability won him the admiration of his colleague, William Knox. Although Pownall held several sinecures and made a tidy fortune out of his long continuance in office, Edmund Burke, arch foe of all such practices, regarded him as an " able intelligent, honest man of remarkable probity." [4] Hillsborough sometimes found him unsteady and temperamental, and the King thought that he was better fitted to carry out the orders of others than to be a military executive.[5]

Pownall's rather pompous manner and his landlady's habit of addressing him as " statesman " aroused the displeasure of Richard Cumberland who worked with him in the Board of Trade.[6] Even Cumberland admitted that if Pownall knew any state secrets he never betrayed them, but he wrote an extremely biassed and inaccurate account of Pownall's dismissal from the Board. The Dartmouth Manuscripts show very clearly that there was no arbitrary dismissal in his case. On the contrary, ever since Dartmouth's appointment in 1772, Pownall had been searching for a less arduous post for " an old worn out troop horse," and his ambition was realized in 1776.[7] Although he resigned his post at the Board of Trade in January, he continued to act as Under-secretary until May, at which time his new position as Commissioner of Excise was confirmed. In 1785 he was appointed Commissioner of Customs. He died ten years later, July 17, 1795, at the age of seventy, leaving his widow, the daughter of Lillingston Bowden Lillingston of Yorkshire, two sons, and a daughter. His elder son became a clerk in the Board of Trade in 1772. The younger, the Honorable George Pownall, was Secretary and member of the Council for Quebec.

Of Major Richard Phelps, who preceded William Knox as junior Under-secretary with Pownall from 1768 to 1770, very little is known.[8] Several volumes of Phelps Correspondence in the Stowe Manuscripts indicate that he had been Secretary to the Embassy at Turin and Under-secretary in the Northern Department from 1745 to February 16, 1768. In all probability the latter date marks the time of his transfer to the American Department.[9] In office, he seems to have been over-shadowed completely by his versatile colleague, and to have confined himself to routine business. In 1769, he became Provost Marshal General of the Leeward Islands, an office which could be filled by deputy, but Pownall succeeded him in that in 1771. Phelps returned to the Northern Department to serve Lord Sandwich when Knox superseded him in the Colonial Office in 1770.

William Knox (1732-1810), who held the post of Under-secretary longer than any of his colleagues, regarded himself as a "principal actor" in the executive government of Great Britain during the American Revolution.[10] Knox was an Irish Protestant by birth, and traced his descent from John Knox, the Scottish reformer. He served his political apprenticeship as Provost Marshal and member of the Council of Georgia, 1756-1761.[11] There he soon became "the favorite" of Governors Henry Ellis of Georgia and Henry Lyttleton of South Carolina, both uncompromising opponents of the colonial claims against Great Britain. When he returned to England in 1761 as Agent for Georgia, Knox had already begun the acquisition of a large colonial estate near Savannah, which eventually included some 8,400 acres and 122 negroes. He carried back to England a distinctly unfavorable impression of the democratic element in the American Colonies.

In England, Knox became known as a colonial expert. He attached himself to George Grenville, whose political views he shared, and in defense of Grenville's imperial policies he assumed the role of pamphleteer. Among his more outstanding pamphlets were *The Claim of the Colonies to an Exemption from Taxation* (1765), which was written to justify the Stamp Act and which cost him his post as Agent for Georgia; *The Present State of the Nation* (1768), which elicited a famous, if somewhat caustic, reply from Edmund Burke; and *The Controversy Between Great Britain and her Colonies Reviewed* (1769), to which Grenville himself made significant contributions. The historians, W. E. H. Lecky and Edward Channing, regarded *The Controversy* as the ablest statement of the case against America.[12] These publications, although they appeared anonymously, soon marked Knox as the leading pamphleteer in support of Parliamentary authority over the Colonies.

When the Colonial Office was established in 1768, Henry Ellis tried in vain to secure for Knox the post which was finally occupied by Richard Phelps. Knox was more successful in 1770, when at the age of thirty-eight, he became joint Under-secretary with Pownall, a post which he retained until the abolition of the Department in 1782. While in office, Knox possessed a singular facility for commending himself to his superiors. In his capacity as Under-secretary, he won the confidence of each successive Secretary of State from Hillsborough to Ellis. George III was well disposed toward him, as well he might be to one who "almost adored" his sovereign. He was on friendly terms with Lord North, who, on more than one occasion, sought his advice on American matters. The active role which he assumed in opposition to the American colonies made him a marked man in the eyes of the liberals of his day.

Knox's services as pamphleteer were now more than ever at the disposal of the Government. In 1774, he published his *Defence of the Quebec Act*. The following year, in an effort to prevent the trading towns of England from siding with the

Americans, he produced *The Interest of the Merchants and Manufacturers of Great Britain in the Present Contest with the Colonies*. During the Revolution he wrote his *Considerations on the State of Ireland* (1778) to further a long cherished project for the relief of Ireland from the commercial restrictions under which she labored. In addition to the heavy responsibilities of his work in the American Department, Knox played an important role in securing the relaxation of the Navigation Acts for Ireland (1778-9).[13]

Just as Knox failed to foresee the Revolution, so also, with blind optimism, he refused to believe in its ultimate success. This lack of foresight cost him his American estates as well as the income from the sinecures he held as Provost Marshal of Georgia and Secretary of New York. He was sufficiently notorious in the Colonies to be hung and burned in effigy in both Boston and Savannah. As a partial compensation for his losses, George III, in 1778, granted him a generous pension of £1200 per year.

When the American Department was abolished in 1782, Knox chose to retire from public life rather than work with Lord Shelburne whom he cordially disliked. During the Fox-North administration in 1783, he returned, at the request of Lord North, to assist without office or emolument in the framing of regulations for the remaining American Colonies.[14] At this time he drafted the Order-in-Council of July 2, 1783, which regulated trade between the United States and the British West Indies and which delayed for some years the breakdown of the old commercial system. Knox believed this to be his most outstanding achievement and he expressed the wish that the document might be engraved upon his tombstone. He also laid the groundwork for the establishment of the Loyalist colony of New Brunswick, a project which was carried out by the next administration largely in accordance with his plans.

The American Revolution terminated Knox's career as a bureaucrat. For the next twenty-seven years he carried on a futile struggle to secure adequate compensation for his losses. His health, never good, was ruined and he became a bitter, meddlesome, and unreasonable old man. For some years he served as Agent for New Brunswick and for Prince Edward Island. He died in 1810. Although he was a man of considerable ability, with a fund of technical knowledge and some literary talent, Knox never understood colonial psychology. The fact that a recognized colonial expert, who had spent five years in America, could be so divorced from reality as to expect the American colonies to submit voluntarily to the doctrine of subordination he prescribed, goes far to explain the American Revolution. As an authorized interpreter of the British conception of colonial dependence he nevertheless merits more consideration than it has in the past fallen to his lot to receive.

Germain appointed Christian D'Oyley as Under-secretary in May, 1776, to succeed John Pownall.[15] D'Oyley was a Whig and an intimate friend of Sir William Howe, the Commander in Chief in America. He was an experienced military executive, having acted as Deputy Secretary at War, a fact which was no doubt responsible for his appointment in the American Department at this time. In the same year he became Commissary General of the Musters and Chief Muster Master of the Forces. D'Oyley was not particularly pleased with the prospect of exchanging his former post of Deputy Secretary at War for the more arduous work of the Colonial Department. Thomas Hutchinson suspected that he wanted as good an income attended by less trouble. The D'Oyleys liked to pass the summer in the country, but as Knox's health obliged him to leave London at that time, they had to remain in the city.

D'Oyley's experience in the War Office led to his being entrusted with a great deal of the military business of the department.[16] Pownall, who seems to have returned temporarily to the American office in November and December, 1776, while Knox was ill, reported that in business his successor was a little like the dog in the manger.[17] Sir William Howe and D'Oyley together prepared the plans and instructions for

Burgoyne's campaign. Knox's now familiar story about D'Oyley's carelessness in neglecting to draft a letter for Germain to notify Howe of his responsibilities toward Burgoyne has for long been generally accepted in assessing the blame for Saratoga.[18] Its significance has recently been discounted, however, by Troyer Steele Anderson, who demonstrates in a convincing manner that if D'Oyley had written such a letter it would not have instructed Howe to give up the Philadelphia campaign in order to effect a junction with Burgoyne's army, since the administration scarcely expected that Burgoyne would need to be rescued.[19]

In February, 1778, at the time of Howe's recall, and probably because of it, D'Oyley abruptly left the American Department, to the surprise and displeasure of Germain.[20] He told Hutchinson that he withdrew because he failed to please Germain, but Hutchinson attributed his resignation to partiality for the Howes. Germain complained to William Eden that D'Oyley's manner of leaving the office was not the most polite, and that he, Germain, was not the first to be informed of it.[21] In 1781, D'Oyley became Comptroller of Army Accounts.

D'Oyley's place was taken by Thomas De Grey, Junior (1748-1818), the only son of the eminent Lord Chief Justice, Sir William De Grey.[22] In 1768, he had been appointed Comptroller of the First Fruits and Tenths of the Clergy. Cumberland refers to his "natural gloom of politics" but there seems to be very little available information about him.[23] As a member of the House of Commons, 1774 to 1780, he sometimes spoke on colonial issues, probably during Germain's absence. In 1779, he defended Germain's right to retain his seat in the House, quoting precedents to prove that the Place Acts of Queen Anne did not exclude the Third Secretary of State from the House.[24] In 1780, he presented an important series of papers on the organization and administration of the Colonial Office to the House.[25] De Grey remained in the American Department for two and a half years. Shortly after his withdrawal in 1780, he succeeded to the title of Baron Walsingham. In 1787, he became Postmaster-General. For some twenty years he acted as chairman of committees in the House of Lords, where he was highly respected. He died on January 16, 1818, at Old Windsor.

Benjamin Thompson (1753-1814), better known by his imperial title, Count Rumford, and as the founder of the Royal Institution of Great Britain, was the most adventurous person in the Colonial Department.[26] He was a native of Massachusetts, and as a young man attended lectures at Harvard College where he displayed an aptitude for science and philosophy. There is reason to believe that during the early stages of the Revolution he acted as a secret agent for General Gage. In 1776, when his estates at Concord, New Hampshire, were confiscated, he left his family and joined the Loyalist emigration to England.

In England, Thompson became the protegé of Germain, who was so favorably impressed that he received him into his family about the time D'Oyley left the office in 1778. Thompson remained in the Colonial Office for a year only. His indiscretion in repeating information that he received from Germain in confidence must have been a source of embarrassment to his chief.[27] As for Thompson, Cuvier claims that he was disgusted with the want of talent displayed by Germain, for which he was not infrequently made responsible.[28] Rufus King, American Minister in England after the Revolution, has asserted that during the war Thompson was guilty of treason, that he was in touch with the notorious spy, La Motte, and was saved from disgrace by the protection of Germain and the death of Lord Suffolk, Secretary for the Northern Department.[29] At the time very little importance seems to have been attached to this episode, and no change took place in the relations of Germain and Thompson. In 1781, Thompson left the department and returned to America to organize the King's American Dragoons from the remnants of the Loyalists on Long Island. At the end of the war he was knighted.

In 1783, after leaving Viscount Sackville [Germain] in charge of his affairs, Thompson set out on his adventures to Bavaria, where he proved so successful in reforming the police system that he received the imperial title of Count Rumford. The British Government refused to receive him as Bavarian Ambassador in London. Some years later, however, he married the widow of the chemist Lavoisier, and returned to England where he founded the Royal Institution of Great Britain.

John Fisher (1745-1811), who succeeded Thompson in the American Department in October, 1781, had been appointed Collector of Customs for Salem and Marblehead, Massachusetts, in 1762, and Naval Officer for New Hampshire in 1765.[30] He likewise acted as Deputy Naval Officer for the ports of Newbury and York. He was a brother-in-law of Governor Wentworth of New Hampshire and had acquired much property in America. As a Customs Collector he was particularly obnoxious to the Revolutionary element in Massachusetts. In October, 1775, his life was threatened, his estates were confiscated, and he was forced to seek refuge in England with his wife and six children.

In England, Fisher was allowed a stipend of £160 per annum in addition to his salary as Collector of Customs. He estimated his loss of income from this post at £566.15.11. His post as Naval Officer had netted him £201.17.7 and he evaluated his American real estate at £25,000.

In 1778, without asking any additional emolument, Fisher returned to America to use the influence he fancied he still possessed to induce the Americans to return to their allegiance. When the futility of his mission became apparent, he returned to England to succeed Thompson in the Colonial Office. There he had particular charge of the cases of American Loyalists seeking compensation for their losses. He had been attached to the Colonial Department for only six months when the office was abolished, but he was fortunate enough to obtain an annuity of £400 in spite of Shelburne's antipathy toward him. Shelburne refused to employ him in the Southern Department. Fisher died at Bath in 1811 at the age of sixty-six, after many fruitless attempts to secure further compensation for loss or devaluation of his American property. He had to provide for a family of twelve children.

Obviously, the Under-secretaries were not lacking in technical training, military, bureaucratic, or both. Three of them had first-hand experience in America, and another, John Pownall, had dealt with American affairs in the Board of Trade for some twenty-seven years before he entered the American Department. The fault lay not in their technical experience, but in their point of view. Three of them, as has already been pointed out, may be classed as American Loyalists, which is in itself sufficient to explain their attitude toward the "rebels," or vice versa, American opinion of them. None of the Under-secretaries took what might be termed a liberal stand on behalf of the Colonies. Both Knox and Pownall were active champions of colonial subordination. It will be recalled that Franklin was too much an American to receive an appointment from the North Administration. The "experts" who threw the weight of their influence on the British side both before and during the Revolution, must, therefore, bear their share of responsibility for the outcome.

---

1 See John Nichols, *Literary Anecdotes of the Eighteenth Century* (London, 1812-16), VIII, 66-7; Cumberland, *Memoirs*, 72-4. The Knox and Dartmouth Manuscripts contain many of Pownall's letters. Nichols lists the following publications by Pownall: "Account of a Roman Tile discovered at Reculver," printed in *Archeologia*, VIII, 79; "Some Sepulchral Antiquities discovered at Lincoln," in *Archeologia*, X, 345; "Admeasurements of the Keeps of Canterbury and Chilham Castles," *Gentlemen's Magazine*, LXIV, 909 (October, 1794). For Pownall's obituary notice, see *ibid.*, LXV, 621-22 (July, 1795).

2 See Basye, *Lords Commissioners of Trade and Plantations*, p. 14 (note).

3 Dartmouth MSS, Box 11, No. 448, "A Londoner" to [Dartmouth], October, 1772.

4 *Parliamentary History*, XXI, 235, 239.

5 *Hist. MSS Comm., Dartmouth MSS* (London, 1887), I, 440; Hutchinson, *Diary*, I, 378, February 17, 1775.

6 Cumberland, *Memoirs*, p. 74.

7 *Ibid.*, p. 202; Dartmouth MSS, No. 487, December 26, 1772; *ibid.*, No. 894, October 12, 1773; *ibid.*, No. 898, October 20, 1773; *ibid.*, No. 1653, January 16, 1776; *ibid.*, No. 1654, January 23, 1776. In 1772, Pownall asked for a post as Governor of Barbados and in 1773 he tried to become one of the Lords of Trade. Germain's letter to Dartmouth of January 23, 1776, reports Pownall's resignation at this time due to the fact that Dartmouth wished the whole arrangement to take place at once.

**8** Brit. Mus., Stowe MSS, Vols. 256-261, Correspondence and papers, political and private, of Major Richard Phelps, Secretary to the Embassy at Turin, and Under-Secretary of State for the Northern Department (February 17, 1745–February 16, 1768).

**9** The Colonial Office correspondence contains letters under his signature at least as early as February 20, 1768. See C. O. 5, Vol. 408, Phelps to Grey Cooper, written according to the directions of Hillsborough.

**10** Wm. Knox, *Extra-Official State Papers*, II, 3-4. The William L. Clements Library of the University of Michigan has eleven volumes of Knox Papers. See also *Dictionary of National Biography* (London, 1885-90), XXXI, 336-37. There is a brief account in Lorenzo Sabine, *Biographical Sketches of Loyalists of the American Revolution* (Boston, 1864).

**11** See Knox Papers, X, 16.

**12** W. E. H. Lecky, *History of England in the Eighteenth Century* (New York, 1903), III, 320; Edward Channing, *History of the United States* (New York, 1924), III, 68-70.

**13** For further discussion, see chap. ix.

**14** Knox Papers, VII, 6, Col. George Augustus North to Knox [May], 1783.

**15** Sackville MSS, 1775-1777, No. 33, Germain to Howe, June 9, 1776. Pownall's fees stopped in May and he no longer participated in interdepartmental correspondence after that month.

**16** See chap. iii, n. 21.

**17** Knox Papers, II, 66, Pownall to Knox, November 13, 1776.

**18** See H. E. Egerton, "Lord George Germain and Sir William Howe," *English Historical Review*, XXV, 315 (April, 1910).

**19** T. S. Anderson, *The Command of the Howe Brothers during the American Revolution* (Oxford, 1936), pp. 256-57.

**20** Hutchinson, *Diary*, II, 184.

**21** Brit. Mus., Add. MSS, 34415, Germain to [Eden], February 10, 1778.

**22** *Gentleman's Magazine*, LXXXVIII, 82-3 (January, 1818), for an obituary notice; *Burke's Peerage* (London, 1930), pp. 2406-407.

**23** Sackville MSS, 1776-1783, Cumberland to Germain (N. D.).

**24** *Parliamentary History*, XX, 266-67.

**25** *Journals of the House of Commons*, XXXVII, 858.

**26** See *Dictionary of National Biography*, LVI, 205-08; Sabine's *Loyalists*, II, 353; R. W. Hale, "Some Account of Benjamin Thompson, Count Rumford," *New England Quarterly*, I, 505-31 (October, 1928); G. E. Ellis, *Memoir of Sir Benjamin Thompson, Count Rumford* (Boston, 1871); Allen French, *General Gage's Informers* (Ann Arbor, 1932).

**27** Hutchinson, *Diary*, II, 337, 339.

**28** G. Cuvier, *Eloges historiques* (Paris, 1860), p. 220.

**29** C. R. King (ed.), *Life and Correspondence of Rufus King* (New York, 1896), III, 518-19, Memorandum Book, September 25, 1801.

**30** On Fisher, see the Audit Office Papers, A. O. 13, Vols. 52 and 73; also Sabine's *Loyalists*, I, 424-25.

# CHAPTER VIII
## THE COLONIAL OFFICE CORRESPONDENCE

THE handling of the Colonial Office correspondence constituted the chief task of the Under-secretaries, one which included the perusal of incoming dispatches, the drafting of outgoing dispatches for the signature of the Secretary of State, and the direct correspondence of the Under-secretaries with colonial officials and with the other departments of the Government. This work was, of course, under the general direction of the American Secretary and the ultimate responsibility for all departmental business rested with him. There was a great deal of routine correspondence, however, only some of which demanded his personal attention, the rest being left to experienced subordinates. When the Secretary was absent, when he was busy with his own private affairs, devoting himself to election propaganda, or as in the case of Germain, attending the House of Commons, the chief responsibility for routine work rested upon the Under-secretaries.

Dartmouth was often absent for days or even weeks, during which time he expected to have no concern with office affairs. Germain, according to William Knox, was inclined to participate only in " capital leading cases." [1] On more than one occasion he congratulated Knox for giving dispatch to so much business without bothering him, and for handling it in such a clear and able manner.[2] Indeed, the Under-secretaries probably knew better than their superiors how to solve such routine problems as that of securing a convoy for the Canada victualling ships and other like matters. Whether the Secretary was in London, Staffordshire, or Drayton, the work of the Department had to be done as efficiently as possible.

It was customary for the Under-secretaries to open and read the official dispatches entering the office, to select information which required the personal attention of the Secretary of State, and to lay it before him. If he were absent in the country for a few days or weeks, one of the Under-secretaries transmitted important intelligence to the Prime Minister, Lord North, laid the dispatches before the King, and sent copies or extracts, as the case demanded, to the absent Secretary. If the letters required no special consideration, the Under-secretary answered them on his own initiative and informed his absent chief of a *fait accompli*.[3] Sometimes he drafted a suitable reply and submitted it for the Secretary's approval.[4] Usually, in the case of important dispatches, he received directions from his chief, drafted his reply accordingly, and submitted it for signature.

Knox seems to have been in the habit of drawing up a precis or abstract of the correspondence to use as a guide in drafting his replies.[5] Some of Pownall's memoranda for letters to colonial Governors are preserved in the Dartmouth Manuscripts.[6] These indicate that specific directions regarding the correspondence must have been supplied by Dartmouth, but that considerable leeway was left to Pownall as far as the form and phraseology were concerned. Germain often gave directions of a most general nature to Knox. In July, 1777, he asked him to say something civil to Governor Tryon of New York for having commanded a successful expedition.[7] On another occasion he asked him to look over that part of the correspondence which he thought would be referred to him, and to have it ready for a conference with Lord North, Amherst, and the Under-secretaries in Suffolk's and Weymouth's departments.[8]

On important issues the Secretary of State often consulted the Prime Minister, the King, or the whole Cabinet before he issued directions for the answering of dispatches, or he submitted the drafts to them before the letters were sent. Pownall prepared the drafts relating to the *Gaspee* affair in August, 1772, as nearly as possible in conformity with what he understood from Dartmouth to be the intention of the King's servants.[9] When Dartmouth approved of them, the King signed the Instructions and read the letters himself. In July, 1778, when Knox was employed to draft a letter to the Commissioners for restoring peace, intimating "in the gentlest manner possible" that they had exceeded their instructions, Germain wished Suffolk, Sandwich, and the whole Cabinet to see the finished product before he signed it.[10]

When the American Secretary was absent, Knox and Pownall sometimes resorted to the head of the Northern or Southern Department to sign dispatches conveying the King's commands.[11] During the stress and strain of the month of September, 1775, Pownall prepared a draft to Governor Legge of Nova Scotia for Dartmouth's signature, but having no time to send it to his chief before the sailing of the packet, he forwarded the unsigned letter to Legge, asking him to stop all proceedings for the escheat of the lands of a certain Mr. Grant until the King's pleasure could be more regularly communicated to him.[12]

Germain seems to have approved in most cases of the drafts submitted to him by Knox and in his replies frequently noted that they were "perfectly right," "very proper," "without exception," or "exactly what I wished."[13] In March, 1776, the King informed Lord North that he was "much pleased" with the letters to Carleton and Burgoyne and that he saw in them "that precision which it would be no disadvantage to other departments if they would imitate."[14] Both Pownall and Knox were capable of writing their dispatches in clear and concise, if not in highly polished language.

When Germain found it necessary to make alterations in the drafts of his Under-secretary, he often expressed the hope that Knox approved or that he didn't mind. In August, 1776, when he omitted part of Knox's draft to Governor Morris of St. Vincent, which he considered too strong, he trusted that Knox would not disapprove.[15] Some of Germain's alterations were quite characteristic. In October, 1776, he made a slight change in Knox's draft to Sir William Howe, as he could not say that he "approved of a cartel with rebels," although he was "glad that the prisoners are to be exchanged."[16]

Germain's relations with Carleton were not the most happy. In September, 1777, he objected to Knox's statement that Haldimand would be sure to obtain valuable information from Carleton with regard to the conduct of the Government at Quebec, and he asked to be absolved from the crime of signing what he did not believe.[17] He had already taken the additional precaution of asking Knox to provide Haldimand with all necessary information about the situation in Canada after the passing of the Quebec Act of 1774.[18]

Although it usually fell to the Secretary to correct the drafts of his subordinate, sometimes the opposite took place. Germain himself drafted a letter to Sir William Howe in response to his request to resign after Burgoyne's surrender at Saratoga. The Knox Papers contain a draft endorsed by Knox himself in the following manner: "Lord G. G.'s paragraph for a letter . . . altered by me in the letter upon that occasion."[19] On December 28, 1780, Germain begged Knox "to correct with attention" what he had hurriedly written to Clinton the day before to enforce the establishment of a post on the Chesapeake, for it was essential in dealing with such a Commander not to give him any opportunity to undertake a foolhardy expedition under the sanction of a positive order. Germain merely wished to convey the impression that such an expedition would be highly desirable whenever circumstances rendered it feasible.[20]

It is impossible to determine, except in a few isolated instances, how much of the contents of the drafts prepared for the signature of the Secretary of State were inspired by the Under-secretaries. The letters of Dartmouth to Pownall and of Germain to Knox afford the only clues to the amount of detail supplied by the Secretaries for the instruction of their subordinates, and these were written during their absence from the office. It can only be assumed that similar conditions prevailed when the Secretaries were present, for there is no record of that aspect of their relations. The Clinton and Sackville Manuscripts contain copies of Germain's letters to Clinton and other colonial officials in the hand of William Knox, and although in these it is fairly safe to assume that Knox himself drafted the letters, there is no indication of what instructions he received.[21] The only conclusion possible is that unless the Secretary accepted the advice of his subordinate, or unless their ideas on colonial issues happened to coincide, the official dispatches reflected the sentiments and opinions of the Secretary and his colleagues rather than those of the Under-secretary. The clerks, as far as can be ascertained, confined themselves to the copying of such correspondence and had nothing to do with the content.

Part of the regular official correspondence between the American Department and colonial officials, as well as that between the American Department and other Government offices, was handled by the Under-secretaries under their own signatures, either on their own initiative or in accordance with directions received from the Secretary of State. By far the greater proportion of this correspondence left the office under the signature of the senior Under-secretary, namely, John Pownall from 1768 to 1776, and William Knox from 1776 to 1782. At one time or another the Under-secretaries had occasion to write to all those officials with whom the Secretaries of State usually corresponded, including the Commanders in Chief in America, the Superintendents of Indian Affairs, and all the colonial Governors. Most of this direct correspondence was occasioned by the absence of the American Secretary or due to his attendance at Cabinet meetings or in the House of Commons.

On the whole, these letters are not particularly significant, and as far as the formulation of policy or the conduct of the Revolutionary War were concerned, they might just as well have been omitted. In many cases Knox and Pownall merely acknowledged that in the absence of the Secretary the dispatches had been received and laid before the King. Often they transmitted intelligence of enemy movements, copies of letters received from other departments, duplicates of former dispatches, copies of Instructions, returns of the German recruits, or the Parliamentary estimates for Colonies like Nova Scotia and Georgia. Occasionally they provided letters of introduction for persons going to the Colonies to serve in some official capacity. The letters of Pownall to Gage and Sir William Howe, and those of Knox to Howe, Clinton, Burgoyne, and Carleton were of a purely formal character.

Even the official correspondence indicates, however, that the Under-secretaries were on personal and friendly terms with several of the colonial Governors and other officials. Colonel Guy Johnson expressed a particular desire to hear occasionally from Knox, whose character he greatly respected.[22] The fact that Knox was selected to inform Haldimand about the Government of Quebec before his departure from England in 1777, may partly account for the number of letters that passed between them during Haldimand's tenure of office.[23] Knox provided Governor Legge of Nova Scotia with a great deal of sound advice about accepting James Monk, Jr., as Attorney-General of that colony in succession to William Nesbitt.[24] There was every reason why he should feel a particular interest in Governor Wright of Georgia who acted as his attorney and manager of his plantations there.[25] With James Simpson, Secretary to the Commissioners for Restoring Peace, Knox corresponded frequently from 1780 to 1782 in a manner which revealed a degree of affinity between the two men on political matters.[26] Knox was confident that Simpson would frustrate any tendency on the part of the Commissioners to guarantee the integrity of the existing colonial constitutions.[27] In his official capacity and apparently with the approbation of Germain, Knox outlined to Simpson and encouraged him to forward one of his own favorite solutions for the colonial problem—the creation of a colonial aristocracy.[28]

The large consignments of Indian presents for North America, especially during the Revolution, occasioned a great deal of correspondence between Under-secretaries Pownall and Knox on the one hand, and the Superintendents of Indian Affairs and Governor Haldimand of Quebec on the other.[29] Most

THE COLONIAL OFFICE CORRESPONDENCE 117

of this concerned the nature, quantity, and quality of the articles needed or received. To have become an expert on the prices and quality of such a varied assortment of goods, which included everything from needles and blankets to silver-mounted pistols, would have been a full-time job for any Under-secretary. Knox, who succeeded Pownall in the management of this business, 1776-1782, was guided principally by the requisitions and suggestions of the Indian agents and Haldimand. In spite of his "fool-proof" system, there were many complaints about the articles forwarded by Knox, due no doubt to the fact that he neglected to have the goods examined before they left England.[30] A lengthy investigation into the whole subject of the expenditures for Indian presents finally resulted in 1784 in the exoneration of Knox from any personal peculation, but indirectly accused him of mismanagement.[31]

The Under-secretaries often dispatched circular letters to the Colonies. These were usually covering notes for the transmission of identical enclosures to several colonial or military officials, often to all the Governors of America.[32] Most of them referred briefly to the enclosure of copies of Acts of Parliament relating to America, copies of the *Gazette* with intelligence of British victories on sea or land, copies of the King's Speech to Parliament and the Address of both Houses in Reply, and copies of Proclamations like that of August, 1775, for the suppression of rebellion and sedition in the Colonies. Circular letters conveying the King's commands were forwarded under the signature of the Secretary of State.

The bulk of the official correspondence from military and colonial officials in America was directed to the Secretary of State rather than to his subordinates. Some of them did not bother to send a separate acknowledgment of letters or intelligence received from the Under-secretaries, particularly if these were of a purely routine nature. Clinton, Gage, and Howe were often content to refer to the receipt of this correspondence in their next dispatches to the Secretary of State.[33] Other officials like Tryon, Penn, Hutchinson, Wright, and Haldimand thought it worth while to tender a direct reply to the most trivial letters from Pownall or Knox. Sometimes colonial or military officials considered it tactful and perhaps advisable to secure the support of the Under-secretary in any attempt to obtain compensation for losses, an increase in salary, or a leave of absence.

Andrew Oliver, Lieutenant-Governor of Massachusetts, who claimed to have had repeated experience of Pownall's friendship, sought his good offices after the publication of the Hutchinson-Oliver correspondence with Whately in 1773, to secure an opportunity to answer the charges brought against him, and in case they proved to have no foundation, " to obtain for him an honourable acquittal." [34] Knox acted as attorney for William De Brahm, Surveyor-General for the Southern District of North America, in obtaining for him a part of the Parliamentary grant of £ 1885.4.0 for the survey of his district.[35] In 1781, General Riedesel expressed his warmest gratitude to Knox " for his obliging readiness to serve the troops of His Serene Highness the Duke of Brunswick." [36] In particular, he acknowledged Knox's assistance in procuring, through Lord George Germain, an allowance equal to forage money for the officers of the Convention Army as compensation for their great losses and extraordinary expenses during the past three years. Knox supervised the forwarding of Haldimand's baggage to him after it had been inadvertently left behind in 1777.[37] In return for Knox's " very kind attention to his interests," especially in relation to his salary as Governor of Jamaica, Sir Archibald Campbell supervised the employment of Knox's negroes, who had been transferred from Georgia to Jamaica at the time of the British evacuation of that province.[38]

On the whole, the letters of colonial officials to the Under-secretaries were of greater significance than those of the Under-secretaries to them. In some cases, of course, they wrote merely to notify the American Secretary indirectly that nothing of importance had occurred since the forwarding of their last dispatches, that troops and food consignments had arrived for the army, or that they had received copies of the Parliamentary estimates and circular letters. Hutchinson of Massachusetts preferred to send the petitions of those who had suffered in Boston for their support of the Crown to Pownall rather than to trouble Hillsborough with every such case, and to leave it to his judgment whether they should be submitted to the Secretary of State.[39]

Hutchinson, Tryon, Wright, and Simpson often included important and interesting comments on colonial conditions in their letters to Pownall and Knox.[40] Sir James Wright wrote things to Knox which he did not consider proper to send direct to Lord George Germain or for the King to see.[41] He relied on Knox's judgment to transmit to his chief any information which it was to Germain's interest to hear. His letters were filled with complaints about the lack of coöperation from the military commanders who resented the restoration of civil government in Georgia. James Simpson was flattered by the willingness of Germain to receive his intelligence through Knox, and he made the most of his opportunity to urge the restoration of civil government in South Carolina.[42] As Germain and Knox were definitely in favor of the restoration of civil government in the Colonies at the earliest opportunity, and the military commanders opposed this step on every occasion, the influence of men like Wright and Simpson may not have been inconsiderable.

Some colonial officials conducted a private correspondence with the Under-secretaries. Letters marked "Private," were essentially unofficial, but the term was constantly misapplied as a substitute for "Secret."[43] When arrangements were being made in February, 1779, to lay the correspondence of Sir William Howe before the House of Commons, Knox notified Captain MacKenzie that he had located four letters marked "Private" in Howe's "Secret" and "Separate" correspondence, the contents of which gave no indication that they were intended to be regarded as unofficial.[44] Germain refused to include them in the report to the House, however, without Howe's consent.

Governors Hutchinson of Massachusetts, Legge of Nova Scotia, and Wentworth of New Hampshire wrote privately to Pownall, while Haldimand of Quebec, Governor Robertson of New York, and Colonel Stuart, Superintendent of Indian Affairs for the Southern Department of North America, corresponded in similar fashion with Knox. Many of these letters were certainly personal in content. Hutchinson wrote privately to Pownall in April, 1773, to relate his troubles in New England, and to provide a personal recommendation for a young Massachusetts inventor, Thomas Danforth, the son of the senior Councillor.[45] Haldimand corresponded privately with Knox about the appointment and emoluments of William Pollock, first clerk in the American Department, as Clerk of the Crown for Quebec, and about the prospects of promotion in Canada for Knox's young nephew, Ensign Battersby.[46] He also forwarded intelligence received from Joseph Galloway about the back posts of Virginia, which he obviously intended to be secret, in the same manner.[47] Governor Robertson of New York thanked Knox personally for his attention to the interests of his family, and explained the steps he had taken in issuing a commission to Samuel Bayard, Knox's deputy in the post of Secretary of New York.[48]

None of the Governors conducted a regular private correspondence with the Under-secretaries. Frequently there was no essential difference in subject matter between letters so labelled and others which were dispatched in the regular official manner and there seems to have been no attempt in England to file them separately.[49] The most that can be claimed for the private correspondence between the Under-secretaries and colonial officials is that in some cases it indicated a close personal relationship, usually based on favors received or anticipated.

The bulk of the interdepartmental correspondence was left to the Under-secretaries to handle under their own signatures, although they usually wrote by the direction of the Secretary of State. Letters conveying the King's commands to the War Office, the Admiralty, the Treasury, and the Board of Ordnance were, of course, dispatched in the Secretary's name, although they were frequently drafted by his subordinates.[50] On the other hand, papers and intelligence transmitted to the Privy Council by the King's command were sent directly by the Under-secretaries according to the directions of their chief.[51] Pownall and Knox during their respective terms as senior Under-secretary handled practically all of the correspondence with the Post Office, the Privy Council, the Customs Board, and the Board of Trade.[52] After the Revolution began, Knox conducted the greater part of the correspondence with the Northern and Southern Departments.[53] It was customary for the Under-secretaries in the American Office to correspond with the Under-secretaries in other departments, but on rare occasions they wrote directly to the Secretary of State or to other department heads.[54]

Germain was inclined to rely on Knox's judgment with regard to the management of interdepartmental business, realizing in all probability that his Under-secretary was more familiar with such matters than he.[55] In July, 1780, he permitted Knox to determine whether his letter to the Board of Ordnance should demand compliance with the requisitions of the Commander in Chief in America for large supplies of artillery for New York and Charleston, or whether the responsibility for the decision should be left to the Board.[56] Knox and Pownall both gave orders to the Post Office for the detention of the packets and for passage for persons en route to America without citing any directions from Dartmouth or Germain.[57]

In the absence of the American Secretary, it was occasionally considered advisable to dispatch interdepartmental correspondence under the signature of one of the other Secretaries. For instance, in the absence of Germain in April, 1777, Weymouth, the Southern Secretary, received and transmitted the Kings' commands to the Admiralty to direct the commander of the convoy for the Hessian and Anspach troops to proceed to America with all speed.[58] Under similar circumstances, Pownall preferred to adopt another method, that of private correspondence, largely due to his dislike of delegating any of the business of the American Office to the other Secretaries. In January, 1776, he sent to Sir Hugh Palliser for his private information a memorandum of preparations to be undertaken at once by the Admiralty without waiting for official directions from Germain, which would follow immediately on his return from the country.[59] This memorandum included directions for provisions for soldiers on three Treasury victualling ships bound for America; orders for frames for three sloops and for as many batteaux as possible for service on Lake Champlain, together with a number of artificers to assemble the parts in Canada; and notice that five convoys must be ready by the end of March to escort five different embarkations of troops, one from Ireland, one from England, one from Scotland, and two from foreign parts. Pownall sent a corresponding memorandum to the Board of Ordnance of the preparations necessary in that department.[60] Upon his return a week later, Germain corroborated all the directions of his subordinate in an official letter.[61] On another occasion, Pownall unofficially advised the Admiralty to direct the transports at Plymouth to proceed directly to Quebec rather than to Cork, and Germain's letter followed the next day.[62]

As the Revolution progressed, there was a marked tendency for the Under-secretary to assume more responsibility during the absence of his superior. In October, 1779, when Germain was out of town, Knox, on his own initiative, notified Stephens, Under-secretary in the Admiralty, that he knew Germain wished the storeships with clothing for the army and Indian presents to proceed to Georgia, and the victualling ships for the navy to go to New York.[63] He ventured to add that the convoy should not be detained for any dispatches unless further information of D'Estaing's operations were obtained. Finally, he thought it his duty to request Stephens to impress upon the Lords of the Admiralty the very great necessity for caution on the part of the commanding officer in approaching the coast of Georgia until he learned of the safety of the Colony.

On another occasion, when Germain was absent in April, 1777, Knox took the liberty to send a private warning to Boddington, head of the Board of Ordnance, of the blame that would fall on his department if the Lord Howe transport were not ready in time to proceed with the foreign troops to New York, and he frankly advised him of what measures he ought to take to arouse the Captains of such ships to a sense of their duty. His letter concluded with a veiled threat about obtaining the King's commands when Germain returned to town if the delay continued.[64] This was not the only occasion on which Knox considered it his duty to upbraid the Board for its inactivity.[65] On the whole, it may be concluded that the private correspondence between the Under-secretaries in different departments was primarily useful as an expedient to prevent delay in the dispatch of military business during the absence of the American Secretary.[66]

Knox's energy and initiative in pushing business through the departments with as little delay as possible received some acknowledgment. When Knox was ill in October, 1779, his friend, Richard Atkinson, lamented that everything had gone wrong since he left the office.[67] In particular, Lord Amherst in the War Office had disavowed the orders of his subordinate concerning the recruits for the West Indies and refused to furnish an adequate number. Atkinson appealed to Knox for the necessary information to finish the business. Germain, in January, 1780, was amazed that a sick man could have worked business through the different departments in the manner Knox had done.[68]

Under-secretaries were in reality confidential secretaries, who were often trusted with a complete knowledge of secret policies and with plans of military operations. They were not all treated equally in this respect, but three of those in the Colonial Department seem to have merited the confidence reposed in them, namely, John Pownall, William Knox, and Thomas De Grey, Junior. Of the first, Richard Cumberland said that if he knew any state secrets he never betrayed them.[69] Knox boasted that a special degree of confidence was placed in him.[70] It was his duty to prepare the orders for warlike preparations, which often passed through many hands, and came under the observation of officials in the Admiralty, Treasury, Ordnance Board, War Office, Navy Board, and Victualling Board. Under these circumstances, it was no easy matter to maintain strict secrecy with respect to prospective military operations. Knox claims to have proposed a plan after the outbreak of the American Revolution which was adopted by Germain with good results. As a result of its adoption, he claimed that not one of "the secret expeditions" was discovered or defeated, and that the preparations for the succor and maintenance of Gibraltar were kept secret. Unfortunately, no copy of this plan is to be found in the Knox or Sackville Manuscripts, and Knox himself contributed no clue as to its location beyond the casual remark that "it will be found where it was my duty to deposit it." [71]

The interdepartmental correspondence affords no conclusive evidence as to the actual operation of the plan other than the labelling of letters concerned with important military projects "Secret," "Most Secret," and "Most Secret and Confidential." In this way they seem to have been kept out of the hands of the clerks, who, apparently, were neither permitted to copy nor to read such correspondence. A separate volume contains the drafts of the secret letters of the American Department from 1778 to 1783, and the Sackville Manuscripts contain a volume labelled "Military Dispatched with Appendix Secret." [72] The Clinton Papers include copies of the secret dispatches of Germain to Clinton in the hand of William Knox.[73]

It was customary, in the absence of the Secretary, for Knox and De Grey to communicate important secret intelligence to the Commanders in Chief in America, the West Indies, and Canada. In January, 1780, Knox considered it his duty to apprize General Vaughan that he must be ready to receive a detachment of troops for the West Indies at an earlier date than he had anticipated.[74] In February, while Germain was attending the House of Commons, Knox sent Vaughan word of the French intention of sending a considerable reinforcement of ships and troops to the West Indies.[75] Germain later commended him for having done all in his power to prevent surprise in North America.[76] Knox informed Haldimand in a " Most Secret " letter of July, 1781, that the French Court had refused to send additional troops to America and that there was, therefore, no further danger of an attack on Canada.[77]

Although Germain claimed that he was in no way consulted about the appointment or instructions of the Commissioners selected in 1778 for the restoration of peace with America, Knox and De Grey were with him when he attended a conference at Lord North's on this subject.[78] Alexander Wedderburn, the Solicitor-General, and William Eden, who became one of the Commissioners, seem to have been largely responsible for the framing of the instructions, but Knox was employed to draft the " Most Secret " letter to Clinton of March 21, 1778, transmitting them, and to produce the final draft of the secret instructions themselves.[79] The copies in the Clinton and Sackville Manuscripts are in his hand.

Unusual precautions were taken in the spring of 1778 to prevent any information about the order for the evacuation of Philadelphia from leaking out. Only the King's most confidential Ministers were informed of it, and Germain was directed to communicate it to no person whatever except his own Under-secretary who was to draft the dispatch.[80] For this Knox was chosen and even De Grey, in whom Germain placed " entire confidence," was not acquainted with the plan. It was probably an accident that the Commissioners themselves left England without hearing of it, an omission which justly aroused the indignation of William Eden.[81] Knox's claim to special confidence was no idle boast.

Precis writers were first appointed in the Home and Foreign

Offices in 1791 at a salary of £ 300 per annum.[82] There was no such official attached to the Colonial Office staff, but similar duties were performed by the Under-secretaries. William Pollock in 1797 explained to the Commissioners on Fees and Gratuities that it was the duty of a person so employed " to abridge all dispatches of importance, whether sent or received, entering them in a book for the purpose of facilitating an immediate reference thereto, either when the originals are occasionally sent out of the office, or when it is deemed unnecessary to consult the more voluminous dispatches themselves." [83]

William Knox claimed that it was his custom to draw up an annual precis of the whole correspondence of the department for the preceding year for the benefit of Cabinet Ministers, each of whom received a copy.[84] A volume of such precis is preserved in the Public Record Office and similar copies can be found in the Knox, Dartmouth, and Sackville Manuscripts.[85] Some of these precis correspond to Knox's description and provide a condensed summary or abstract of the incoming and outgoing letters for the year. There was a separate precis of interdepartmental correspondence for 1775, supplemented by another of American correspondence during the same period.[86] On the other hand, the precis of September, 1778, to October, 1779, included both types of letters arranged chronologically.[87]

Precis of correspondence on special topics were sometimes prepared, particularly on various aspects of military operations during the American Revolution. These included a " Precis of Operations on the Canadian Frontier from September 4, 1774, to October, 1776," presumably by William Knox, a " Precis of Measures relative to the Expedition sent against the Southern Provinces in 1775 and particulars of its failure," " A State of Sir Wm. Howe's Army Campaign, 1777," and a " Precis of Transactions on the Mississippi, 1778." [88] The contents of Knox's precis of correspondence with Clinton from March 8, 1778, to December 4, 1779, were considered confidential, for the document was endorsed as follows: " To be copied in a large black hand and to be kept secret." [89] Occasionally, abstracts were made of the precis themselves, as in the case of those by Knox for 1777 and 1778.[90] All of the precis, both general and particular, were objective in character and there seems to have been no attempt on the part of the writer to express his own sentiments about any order or military operation, whether success or failure was the outcome.

Some of the precis proved particularly useful. In December, 1773, Pownall requested Knox to lighten his burdens by undertaking to prepare, for Lord North's information, a precis of the affairs of Quebec from 1763 to date, with special reference to the claims and complaints of the French Canadians and the measures taken to conciliate them.[91] This was intended to provide the necessary background for the preparation of the Quebec Act of 1774. It is probable that the Ministers with such an abstract at their disposal rarely turned to the original documents for information. Knox, himself, perhaps due to the precis, was regarded henceforth as an authority on Canada, and in 1777 he was chosen to inform Governor Haldimand about the situation there after the passing of the Quebec Act.[92] On another occasion, probably during the Loyalist migration to Canada at the close of the Revolution, Germain found Knox's precis a valuable source of information about the state of that province.[93]

After Saratoga, when the Burgoyne expedition was made the subject of Parliamentary inquiry, Thurlow, the Attorney-General, approached Knox to learn what he could of the motives and reasons back of the expedition, the steps taken to put it into execution, and the causes of its failure.[94] Knox promptly produced a copy of his precis of operations for 1776 and 1777, which Thurlow said was "the very thing he wanted." When he learned that the Ministers all had copies, he asserted that they had in that case never read them "for not one of them knew a tittle of the matter." Thurlow's satisfaction with the precis was the beginning of an association between the two men which became more intimate in later years.

During the Revolutionary War, it was the "peculiar duty"

of William Knox "to procure information of the enemy's condition in every part and to point out those in which they might be attacked with the greatest advantage." [95] Intelligence poured in upon him from every department of the Government, particularly from the other two Secretaries, the Treasury, Customs, Post Office, and Admiralty. Colonial officials, especially the military commanders, Governors, and Superintendents of Indian Affairs, contributed their quota of information. Even before the Revolution began, the letters of persons suspected of pro-American sympathies were tampered with. While Hillsborough was still in office, Franklin found that letters from his son, Governor Franklin of New Jersey, and those from the Assembly of Massachusetts Bay, whose agent he then was, were opened. He fancied that the unusual practice of rubbing them open was due to the ingenuity of Mr. Secretary Knox! [96] When the war began, the volume of intercepted correspondence increased considerably.[97]

As far as can be ascertained, most of the secret service activity in England was handled by the two "ancient" Secretaries. It is possible that some of the £3000 received by the American Secretary for this purpose was spent on securing the services of secret agents, but it seems more likely that this sum was regarded as a part of the Secretary's salary. Pownall, in September, 1775, preferred to wash his hands of treasonable business by transmitting all "the strange information" he had accumulated about a certain Mr. Leslie in an official letter to Sir Stanier Porten in the Southern Department.[98] Knox, however, exulted over the fact that he was instrumental in effecting "the only vigorous act of the late administration" against the abettors of the Revolution in England by the seizure in 1779 of Captain Hutchins and his papers without any warrant at all, and "in defiance of all the bad law, and factious oratory that had been bellowed out against *general warrants.*"[99] Hutchins was imprisoned and the fright he was in utilized to the full by the American Department to procure information. Knox seems to have employed him in decyphering letters.[100]

A very extraordinary incident occurred in 1781 as a result of Rodney's victory at St. Eustatius. Having seized a considerable number of papers containing evidence of a contraband trade between the Americans and the Dutch, Rodney shipped them to England for the information of the American Secretary, together with two prisoners by the name of Gouverneur and Curzon, whose correspondence with John Adams, the American agent in Holland, implicated them in the trade.[101] On their arrival in London, the prisoners became "the particular charge" of William Knox, who, as a Justice of the Peace for Middlesex, was present at their examination for high treason before Sir Sampson Wright at the American Office on July 27, 1781.[102] Gouverneur and Curzon were imprisoned and no person permitted to have access to them without a special order from Knox himself. Their papers were retained in the Secretary's office, together with a second consignment from Rodney of a similar nature. By the directions of Knox, Benjamin Thompson, with the assistance of two American Loyalists, made a precis of the second batch of papers which were then placed in charge of William Pollock, the chief clerk.

When it became evident in March, 1782, that the case against Gouverneur and Curzon would soon be dismissed, Knox, fearing that he might be prosecuted for his share in their confinement, helped himself to that part of the correspondence which contained the chief evidence of their guilt without consulting anyone.[103] In 1786, the House of Lords, during consideration of a Bill for the investment of the produce of the St. Eustatius capture in the hands of trustees, conducted an investigation into the removal of the papers from the American Office.[104] From the evidence placed before the House, it appears that Knox still retained in his custody the papers he had seized in 1782, but that at least part of the others belonging to Richard Jennings were surrendered in January, 1783, by an order of the Home Secretary. It seems likely that Knox surrendered the papers of Gouverneur and Curzon at this time for they are not in the Knox Manuscripts. His extraordinary conduct in secreting the correspondence without authority was the subject of comment in a letter to the *Gentleman's Magazine,* published in response to his obituary notice.[105]

The handling of the Colonial Office correspondence directed the attention of the Under-secretaries to a great variety of subjects. Moreover, it seems evident, that with the exception of issues of outstanding importance, the routine business rested largely on their shoulders. They would have been versatile, indeed, had they been experts in every phase of their activities. Strangely enough, in view of the voluminous nature of the correspondence which passed through their hands, John Pownall was able to act not only as Under-secretary in the American Department, but as Secretary of the Board of Trade, 1768-1776. Likewise, William Knox, in addition to the heavy responsibilities imposed on the Under-secretary by the Revolution, found it possible to handle the consignments of Indian presents, 1776-1782, and to carry on an extensive extra-official correspondence with Irish officials for the relaxation of the commercial restrictions under which Ireland still labored in 1778.

---

1 Knox Papers, II, 66, Pownall to Knox, November 13, 1776.

2 See, for example, Knox Papers, V, 22, Germain to Knox, January 8, 1780; *ibid.,* VI, 1, Germain to Knox, January 1, 1781.

3 Sackville MSS, Home Affairs, 1751-1784, Knox to Germain, September 6, 1780.

4 For example, see Dartmouth MSS, Box 18, No. 760, Pownall to Peter Michell, December, 1773. This letter is enclosed in a wrapper containing the following note in Pownall's hand: "The inclosed letter consequential of the advices lately rec'd from America is submitted to your Lordship and shall either be sent or suppress'd as you think fit."

5 Knox, *Extra-Official State Papers,* I, 34. Knox gave Shelburne his precis by which he intended to answer the Quebec dispatches of 1781.

6 Dartmouth MSS, Box 18, No. 768 [N. D. 1773], Notes for Letters to American Governors.

7 Knox Papers, III, 18, Germain to Knox, July 1, 1777.

8 *Ibid.,* IV, 51, Germain to Knox, January 7, 1779.

9 Dartmouth MSS, Box 10, No. 397, Pownall to [Dartmouth], August 27, 1772.

10 Knox Papers, IV, 18, Germain to Knox, July 26, 1778.

11 See, for example, *ibid.,* I, 54, Pownall to Knox, September 26, 1772; C. O. 5, Vol. 254, p. 134, Weymouth to the Lords of the Admiralty, April 3, 1777.

## THE COLONIAL OFFICE CORRESPONDENCE 131

12 C. O. 218, Vol. 25, p. 216, Pownall to Legge, September 18, 1775.

13 See, for example, the following letters of Germain to Knox in the Knox Papers, III, 9, 23, 27, 44; IV, 41, 59; V, 21.

14 *Correspondence of George III and Lord North*, II, 16, No. 349, The King to North, March 30, 1776.

15 Knox Papers, III, 23, Germain to Knox, August 4, 1777; another example occurs in IV, 27, where Germain in altering a draft by Knox to the Commissioners for restoring peace and to Clinton, says, "I hope you will approve."

16 *Ibid.*, II, 58, Germain to Knox, October 19, 1776.

17 *Ibid.*, III, 39, Germain to Knox, September 19, 1777.

18 *Ibid.*, III, 36, Germain to Knox, September 6, 1777.

19 *Ibid.*, IX, 25 [February, 1778]; see also, C. O. 5, Vol. 94, pp. 51-2, Germain to Howe, No. 25, February 4, 1778.

20 Knox Papers, V, 65, Germain to Knox, December 29, 1780; Welbore Ellis expected similar assistance from Knox. Shortly after assuming office, he wrote to him as follows: "I send you some lines which I have very hastily strung together this morning for your correction & if they can be of any use for being incorporated with your own—I am a total stranger to these things & shall take it unkindly if you prefer politeness to the sincerity & assistance of a real friend and adviser in my publick duty." *Ibid.*, VI, 39.

21 See for example, Clinton MSS, Vol. 146, Germain to Clinton, June 5, 1778; *ibid.*, March 21, 1778; *ibid.*, Vol. 148, March 15, 1780.

22 C. O. 5, Vol. 229, Col. Guy Johnson to Knox, July 10, 1777.

23 The Haldimand Papers (Canadian Archives Transcripts) contain numerous letters between Knox and Haldimand. Some of them concern Indian presents.

24 Dartmouth MSS, No. 1064, Knox to Legge, November 2, 1774.

25 Audit Office Papers, A. O. 12, Vol. 4, p. 3. Knox intended to marry Wright's daughter, who was drowned during an Atlantic voyage.

26 The Commissioners for Restoring Peace corresponded regularly with the American Department. Knox himself corresponded with the Secretaries to the Commissioners, Adam Ferguson and James Simpson. See C. O. 5, Vols. 177-78, 180-81. Germain seems to have relied on Knox for drafting most of his dispatches to the Commissioners. When Knox was absent in October, 1778, Germain remarked that they must do the best they could in answering letters from Clinton and the Commissioners in his absence. See Knox Papers, IV, 38.

27 C. O. 5, Vol. 178, p. 219, Knox to Simpson, March 1, 1781.

28 See, for instance, Sackville MSS, Miscellaneous and Undated, "Considerations on the great Question, what is fit to be done with America?"

29 See *supra*, chap. iii, pp. 56-7; Haldimand Papers (Canadian Archives Transcripts), 1776-1782.

30 Treasury Papers, T 1, Vol. 573, Comptrollers' Report on Account of Goods provided by William Knox, Esq., &c., July 12, 1782.

31 Audit Office Papers, A. O. 17, Vol. 56, p. 308, Comptrollers' Report to the Lords of the Treasury relative to the Indian Presents purchased by Mr. Knox in 1782 [July 20, 1784].

32 The circular letters can be found in C. O. 5, Vols. 241 and 242.
33 Several examples can be found in *ibid.*, Vols. 235-37.
34 *Ibid.*, Vol. 762, p. 715, Oliver to Pownall, June 28, 1773. Whately was the secretary of George Grenville.
35 Treasury Papers, T 1, Vol. 479, Memorial of Wm. De Brahm [In Knox's hand], 1770. The memorial is signed in the name of De Brahm by his Attorney, Will. Knox.
36 C. O. 42, Vol. 41, Riedesel to Knox, September 29, 1781.
37 Haldimand Papers (Canadian Archives Transcripts), B. 43, p. 37, Knox to Haldimand, May 15, 1778; C. O. 42, Vol. 38, Haldimand to Knox, October 24, 1778.
38 Knox Papers, VI, 54, Campbell to Knox, September 15, 1782.
39 C. O. 5, Vol. 759, p. 539, Hutchinson to Pownall, August 29, 1770.
40 *Ibid.*, Vol. 246, Hutchinson to Pownall, January, 1773; *ibid.*, Vol. 1108, p. 239, Tryon to Knox, April 21, 1777; *ibid.*, Vol. 176, p. 508, Wright to Knox, February 23, 1782; *ibid.*, Vol. 178, p. 343, Simpson to Knox, July 28, 1781; *Ibid.*, p. 377, Simpson to Knox, August 20, 1781.
41 *Ibid.*, Vol. 176, p. 504, Wright to Knox, February 16, 1782.
42 *Ibid.*, Vol. 230, Simpson to Knox, December 31, 1780; *ibid.*, Simpson to Knox, August 20, 1781; *ibid.*, Vol. 178, p. 343, Simpson to Knox, July 28, 1781; *ibid.*, p. 377, Simpson to Knox, August 20, 1781.
43 See Thompson, *op. cit.*, p. 98, where he says, "'Private' letters, in fact, seem merely to have been especially confidential communications and also—sometimes—less formal and official documents than the regular dispatches." William Knox certainly understood that private letters were unofficial, and that the word "private" was meant to convey a different meaning from that of "secret" for which it was often used. See C. O. 5, Vol. 251, Knox to Captain Mackenzie, February 25, 1779.
44 *Ibid.*, Vol. 251, Knox to Captain Mackenzie, February 25, 1779.
45 Dartmouth MSS, No. 851, Hutchinson to Pownall, April 19, 1773.
46 Haldimand Papers (Can. Archives), B. 55, p. 50, Haldimand to Knox, June 14, 1781 (Private). However, he wrote a long letter to Knox on the subject of Battersby which was not marked "Private". *Ibid.*, B 66, p. 218.
47 C. O. 42, Vol. 40, Haldimand to Knox (Private), October 25, 1780. (See Haldimand Papers, B 55, p. 15, where the date is given as the 24th).
48 C. O. 5, Vol. 1110, p. 301, Robertson to Knox (Private), September 21, 1780.
49 They are, on the contrary, filed indiscriminately with the regular correspondence in most cases.
50 For example, Knox Papers, III, 6, 40, 52; *ibid.*, VI, 31. The Knox Papers contain the covering sheet of a draft endorsed as follows by Knox: "Lord Sandwich having shown Mr. Knox the minute of Cabinet of the 10th inst., he prepared a letter in consequence and sent it down to Lord George Germain, who has returned it signed, with orders to send it to the Admiralty if your Majesty approves of the draft." January 14, 1782.

## THE COLONIAL OFFICE CORRESPONDENCE 133

51 C. O. 5, Vol. 133, contains drafts of the out-letters from the American Department to the Privy Council.

52 For the Post Office, see *ibid.*, Vols. 247-9, In-Letters, and Vols. 250-2, Out-Letters. For the Customs correspondence, see *ibid.*, Vols. 146-9. For the Board of Trade, see *ibid.*, Vols. 241-251.

53 *Ibid.*, Vols. 138-144.

54 *Ibid.*, Vol. 161, Pownall to Townshend, August 3, 1775. Pownall on this occasion wrote in the absence of Dartmouth and by his directions to the head of the Board of Ordnance, signifying that the King approved sending another engineer or even two to America. He added that an official letter would be sent if necessary. Apparently the Board demanded an official communication, for on October 14, 1775, Suffolk signified the King's commands for sending an engineer to Halifax. See also C. O. 325, Vol. 2, Pownall to Suffolk, October 19, 1773.

55 Knox Papers, V, 41, Germain to Knox, July 30, 1780; also, *ibid.*, V, 35, Germain to Knox, April 29, 1780, where Germain acknowledges that Knox knew better than he or Sandwich how to solve the problem of securing a convoy for the Canada victualling ships.

56 *Ibid.*, V, 41, Germain to Knox, July 30, 1780.

57 There are numerous examples in C. O. 5, Vol. 251.

58 *Ibid.*, Vol. 254, p. 134, Weymouth to the Lords of the Admiralty, April 3, 1777.

59 *Ibid.*, Vol. 254, p. 5, Pownall to Sir Hugh Palliser (Private), January 1, 1776.

60 *Ibid.*, Vol. 162, Pownall to Boddington (Private), January 7, 1776.

61 *Ibid.*, Vol. 254, p. 7, Germain to the Lords of the Admiralty, January 15, 1776; *ibid.*, p. 8, January 15, 1776.

62 *Ibid.*, p. 45, Pownall to Stephens, March 6, 1776; *ibid.*, p. 51, Germain to the Lords of the Admiralty, March 19, 1776.

63 *Ibid.*, p. 304, Knox to Stephens, October 23, 1779.

64 *Ibid.*, Vol. 163, p. 195, Knox to Boddington (Private), April 1, 1777.

65 *Ibid.*, Vol. 165, p. 531, Knox to Boddington, October 17, 1780.

66 In the Brit. Mus., Add. MSS, 34413, there is a letter from Knox to William Eden, dated April 10, 1777, requesting information with respect to the embarkation figures for the Brunswick troops. He apologized "for all these enquiries extra-officially" as he needed the reply at once and no time must be lost.

67 Knox Papers, V, 15, R. Atkinson to Knox, October 28, 1779.

68 *Ibid.*, 22, Germain to Knox, January 8, 1780.

69 Cumberland, *Memoirs*, p. 74.

70 Knox, *Extra-Official State Papers*, I, 15-16.

71 *Ibid.*, p. 16.

72 C. O. 5, Vol. 263; On the other hand, the files of the regular correspondence also contain some letters marked "Secret" as in the case of *ibid.*, Vol. 97, p. 707, Germain to Clinton, June 25, 1779. It is possible that these files were completed after the necessity for secrecy no longer existed.

**73** Clinton Papers, Vol. 146, Germain to Clinton, March 21, 1778 (Most Secret).
**74** C. O. 5, Vol. 263, p. 112, Knox to Vaughan, January 6, 1780.
**75** Sackville MSS, Military Dispatched with Appendix Secret, Knox to Vaughan, February 10, 1780.
**76** Knox Papers, V, 33, Germain to Knox, March 29, 1780.
**77** C. O. 5, Vol. 263, pp. 230-31, Knox to Haldimand (Most Secret), July 31, 1781.
**78** Knox Papers, X, 34, Lord Thurlow. See also Sackville MSS, Letters to General Irwin, 1761-1784, Germain to Irwin, February 3, 1778.
**79** Clinton Papers, Vol. 146, Germain to Clinton, March 21, 1778; Knox Papers, IV, 12, Germain to Knox [March, 1778?]; Sackville MSS, America & Miscellaneous, 1775-1782, contain a copy of the secret instructions to the Commissions in Knox's hand.
**80** Brit. Mus., Add. MSS, 34415, f. 452, Germain to Eden, July 31, 1778; another copy in Sackville MSS, America, 1778, No. 51ª; Steven's *Facsimiles*, V, No. 513, Lt. Col. Ed. Smith to Eden [May-August, 1778].
**81** *Ibid.*
**82** *Reports from Committees of the House of Commons*, XII, "Sixteenth Report from the Select Committee on Finance," Appendix M, p. 325; Examination of William Pollock.
**83** *Ibid.*, p. 301.
**84** Knox Papers, X, 25, Lord Thurlow.
**85** C. O. 5, Vol. 253; also *ibid.*, Vol. 232; Sackville MSS, Supplementary, Vol. 1, "Abstract of Precis, 1777 and 1778"; *ibid.*, America, 1778, "Precis of Transactions on the Mississippi"; *ibid.*, America, 1779, "Precis of Orders, 1778, 1779"; Knox Papers, IX, 26, "Precis of Correspondence with Clinton, March 8, 1778, to December 4, 1779"; Dartmouth MSS, No. 1701, Knox to Dartmouth, August 22, 1776, enclosing "Intelligence from America, August, 1776," a Precis of news from Sir Peter Parker.
**86** See Sackville MSS, Supplementary, Vol. 1, "Minutes of Lord Dartmouth's Correspondence with the other Offices and King's Servants, 1775." This seems to have been part of a much more extensive Precis of the entire correspondence of the American Department for the year 1775. See *Hist. MSS Comm., Dartmouth MSS*, II, 410, which includes the correspondence of Dartmouth with General Gage; the circular letters to the Governors; the correspondence with the Governors of the different provinces of Quebec, Massachusetts, New Hampshire, New York, New Jersey, Virginia, Maryland, Pennsylvania, Rhode Island, Connecticut, North and South Carolina, Georgia, Plantations General and Indian Agents (275 pages).
**87** C. O. 5, Vol. 178, pp. 1 *et seq.*, "Precis of Correspondence in the American Department, 1779" (62 pages).
**88** See Sackville MSS, America & Miscellaneous, 1774-1782, and another copy of the same in C. O. 5, Vol. 253; *ibid.*, Vol. 232, pp. 379 ff.; *ibid.*, Vol. 253, No. 9; Sackville MSS, America, 1778, No. 78. Both copies of the "Precis of Operations on the Canadian frontier" contain corrections and additions in Knox's hand. The "Precis of Measures relative to the

THE COLONIAL OFFICE CORRESPONDENCE 135

Expedition sent against the Southern Provinces" is apparently by Knox. See his letter to Dartmouth, August 22, 1776, in the Dartmouth MSS, No. 1701. The "State of Sir William Howe's Army Campaign, 1777," is in Knox's hand, as is also the "Precis of Transactions on the Mississippi."

89 Knox Papers, IX, 26.

90 Sackville MSS, Supplementary, Vol. 1, "Abstract of Precis, 1777 and 1778"; C. O. 5, Vol. 7, contains a document labelled "Abridged Precis, 1777," in Knox's hand.

91 Knox Papers, II, 4, Pownall to Knox, December 3, 1773. Pownall added, "You know how little able I am to sit down to such a work and you know that nobody but you or I can do it."

92 *Ibid.*, III, 36, Germain to Knox, September 6, 1777.

93 Knox, *Extra-Official State Papers*, II, Appendix 23, p. 84, Germain to Knox, November 19, 1789. The date must be incorrect for Germain died in 1785.

94 Knox Papers, X, 25, Lord Thurlow.

95 *Ibid.*, VIII, 6, Knox to Pitt, May 30, 1790.

96 Smyth, *Franklin*, V, 461 ff., B. Franklin to W. Franklin, December 2, 1772.

97 See, for example, C. O. 5, Vol. 40 (1770-1777).

98 Dartmouth MSS, No. 1500, Pownall to Dartmouth, September 7, 1775.

99 Knox, *Extra-Official State Papers*, I, 22.

100 Knox Papers, V, 8, Germain to ———, August 29, 1779; C. O. 5, Vol. 7, Thomas Hutchins to Knox, September 16, 1779; also, Knox Papers, V, 13, 14.

101 Sackville MSS, America, 1781-2, No. 23, Rodney to Germain (Private), March 4, 1781; C. O. 5, Vol. 160, p. 305, Germain to the Attorney & Solicitor General, July 5, 1781; *ibid.*, p. 316, Report of the Attorney & Solicitor General on the case of Gouverneur & Curzon, July 21, 1781; *ibid.*, Vol. 152, Knox to the Attorney & Solicitor General, July 27, 1781.

102 Knox, *Extra-Official State Papers*, I, 39.

103 *Journals of the House of Lords*, XXXVII, 562-64, July 5, 1786.

104 *Ibid.*; see also, Shelburne MSS, Vol. 84, f. 52, State of the Case of the Removal of the St. Eustatius Papers from the Office of the Secretary of State.

105 *Gentleman's Magazine*, October, 1810, pt. ii, p. 320, a letter signed "S. H." No further action seems to have been taken with regard to the St. Eustatius Papers. As Shelburne wrote to Sydney (Shelburne Papers, Vol. 84, f. 64), "This evidence does not seem in the least to apply to the bill before the House, but seems to consist of a voluntary communication of his (Mr. Knox's) opinion of the administration of 1782." In view of Knox's action, it is strange to find him proposing the following resolution for Parliamentary adoption: "That all original papers, of a public nature, that are received into any of the public offices, are the property of the Crown; and that to remove them, or destroy them, without His Majesty's command, is a high misdemeanor." *Extra-Official State Papers*, I, 13-14. There are some Gouverneur and Curzon papers in C. O. 5, Vol. 1235.

## CHAPTER IX
## THE UNDER-SECRETARY AND COLONIAL POLICY

POLITICAL scientists of the past two decades have been diligent in pointing out the dangers of bureaucracy and its growing influence under a regime of dictatorship or democracy. Due to the fact that political appointees remain in office for a limited time and are subject to removal as a result of a sudden or periodic shift in the party kaleidoscope, permanent officials have often enjoyed an advantage over their superiors not only in the management of departmental business but also in the shaping of policies. In the eighteenth century American Department, as we have already seen, the Under-secretaries in practice retained office irrespective of the removal of the Secretary of State.[1] It would be presumptuous to assume that because of these circumstances they moulded colonial policy from 1768 to 1782. To disregard the influence of the "experts," which has been the tendency in the past, may be equally short-sighted. The "Londoner" who warned Dartmouth against the reactionary influence of his two Under-secretaries, John Pownall and William Knox, was not the only person aware of the dependence of the Colonial Secretary upon information and advice supplied by his subordinates.[2] Benjamin Franklin's satisfaction at the appointment of Dartmouth in 1772 was qualified by the fact that he retained the services of the same Under-secretaries who would probably remind him of former measures and prompt him to continue them.[3] John Almon, the publisher, attributed many of the unfortunate measures against America to the "zeal and suggestions" of Knox.[4] In this chapter some attempt will be made to guage the influence of the two most outstanding experts of the American Department, Pownall and Knox.

Much of the influence of an Under-secretary depended, of course, upon the state of his relations with his superior. Because Knox disagreed with Hillsborough, Sir Francis Bernard, and John Pownall in 1770 over proposed alterations in the charter of Massachusetts, he was "ever after excluded by Lord Hillsborough from all consultations whilst he staid in office."[5] In other cases, however, the relations of the Secretary and his subordinate were friendly and even intimate in character. Pownall's letters expressed genuine affection for Dartmouth, and he exerted himself to the utmost to preserve his chief from worry and annoyance.[6] He was so confident of Dartmouth's esteem that he ventured to open one of his private letters from Burgoyne and to forward a copy of it for Lord North's information.[7] During Dartmouth's extended absence in September, 1775, Pownall did not hesitate to remind him in courteous terms that any further delay in his return would be irreconcilable with his duty as Secretary of State.[8] Germain had such confidence in Knox as a colonial expert that he habitually sent those who sought information on Ireland or America to him for advice.[9] Even socially, they were on terms approaching intimacy. Germain sent partridges to Knox from his country home at Stoneland, and they invited one another to turtle dinners. He later consented to act as godfather to one of Knox's sons. Since Lord North "had a kindness" for Knox and "used to talk confidentially with him," Germain sometimes chose to use his subordinate as intermediary in his relations with the Prime Minister. When he could no longer endure the state of uncertainty over his approaching resignation in January, 1782, he sent Knox to Lord North to learn the verdict and remarked later to the King that, in view of the relations between him and his Under-secretary, it was the same as if he had gone himself.[10]

During the years prior to the Revolution, there is less definite proof of the efforts of the Under-secretaries to influence colonial policy. At this time, the authority of the Colonial Office was continually challenged by the "ancient" Secretaries.[11] Owing to the frequent absence of Dartmouth, Pownall sometimes found that colonial business was deflected into other channels. The lack of any Pownall Papers to parallel the Knox Papers for this period is unfortunate. In view of Pownall's aggressive attitude toward the encroachment of the other departments and his long experience as Secretary of the Board of Trade, it seems hardly likely that he would play a passive role in matters of policy. The limited materials available in the Knox and Dartmouth Manuscripts indicate that he was probably as active in giving advice as in managing the routine work of the office.

There is every reason to believe that both Pownall and Knox considered it part of their business, in fact an obligation and a duty, to advise their superiors. As Knox once explained, the only reason he did not have occasion to warn Hillsborough against the westward expansion of the American colonies, was because the Colonial Secretary was as anxious as he to prevent it.[12] Hillsborough seems to have been in the habit of conferring with his Under-secretaries on colonial problems. During one of these sessions in 1770 over the disturbed state of Massachusetts, Hillsborough, Pownall, and Sir Francis Bernard, former Governor of Massachusetts, favored the closing of the port of Boston, the regulation of juries, the end of town meetings, and alterations in the colonial Council.[13] Knox himself opposed all measures other than the changes in the Council, presumably intended to increase its authority and make it more aristocratic. It was due to his dissent on this occasion that Hillsborough neglected to consult him in the future. Knox is authority for the statement that Pownall originally recommended the Boston Port Bill of 1774,[14] soon to be known as one of the five intolerable acts. Letters in the Dartmouth Manuscripts likewise suggest that Pownall was responsible for the removal of Lord Charles Montagu from South Carolina [15] and the recall of Thomas Hutchinson from Massachusetts in 1773.[16] During the boundary dispute between New York and New Hampshire in the same year, both Pownall and Knox combined to urge Dartmouth to refuse the request of Governor Tryon of New York for the assistance of troops against the New Hampshire rioters.[17] Again in August, 1775, they made a joint and apparently successful effort to impress Dartmouth and North with the necessity for issuing a Proclamation for the suppression of the rebellion.[18] Both Knox and Pownall were strong exponents of the theory of colonial dependence and Parliamentary supremacy over the American Colonies.

There is a statement in the Knox Papers in a document entitled "Proceedings in relation to the American Colonies," which suggests in terms which are unfortunately vague, that Knox and Pownall were consulted upon Lord North's Conciliatory Motion of 1775, as well as upon the Address to the King during the same session.[19] In this document, Knox states that Pownall, with his assistance, drafted "the American clause," presumably the Conciliatory Motion itself, and that the speech upon it was the only one on which they were ever consulted. Knox likewise claims to have made some amendments to the Address which was submitted to him by Sir Grey Cooper, Secretary of the Treasury.

There are, however, other reasons for believing that Knox, at least, had something to do with the Conciliatory Motion. On the eve of its introduction in the House of Commons in February, 1775, Knox was in correspondence with John Blackburn, Chairman of the London merchants trading with America.[20] He had apparently discussed with Blackburn a plan by which he intended to provide at one and the same time for imperial defense and for the security of the Colonies against unlimited taxation by Parliament. This plan contemplated yielding the right of taxation by Parliament as long as the Colonies contributed their quota to imperial defense. It was the same proposal which Knox had intended to include in *The Present State of the Nation* in 1768 but which he deleted at Grenville's request.[21] Knox claimed that he had already suggested his scheme to "some Great Men" and that it had met their approbation.[22]

In addition to the general principle mentioned above, Knox proposed in some detail a method for raising money in the Colonies to provide for defense. He recommended that the Colonies pass acts levying a poundage duty on all exports and foreign imports, the proceeds of which were to be placed at the disposal of Parliament as the colonial quota toward imperial defense, while the Colonies in addition assumed the responsibility of providing for their own civil government.[23] These acts were to go into effect whenever Parliament removed the duties on tea and wines imported into the Colonies, and were to remain in force as long as Parliament refrained from levying taxes or duties on the Colonies for any purpose other than the regulation of trade. In the event of war, Knox advocated a requisition by the King as preferable to taxation by Parliament.

During the debate on the Conciliatory Motion in the House of Commons, Colonel Barré, a bitter opponent of the measure, exclaimed: "How this new scheme of letting Americans tax themselves, ever came into the noble lord's [Lord North] head, I cannot conceive."[24] He very much doubted if it was a genuine product of Lord North's wisdom and broadly hinted that it savored of Grenville's policy of *divide et impera*. There is no conclusive evidence to indicate that Knox was the real author of the Conciliatory Motion. That Motion did not recommend any duties on colonial imports or foreign exports, although it corresponded with the general principle set forth in Knox's letter to Blackburn on February 15, 1775, the same general principle which Knox had been ready to concede in 1768, had not Grenville then regarded such action as "the highest species of treason" to the nation.[25] No doubt the reception of this appeasement program in the Colonies was sufficient to repress Knox's enthusiasm for letting Americans tax themselves. He later alleged that the vagueness of the Conciliatory Motion, which specified neither the sum nor the proportion the colonies were to pay, was responsible for its failure.[26]

UNDER-SECRETARY AND COLONIAL POLICY 141

Although Knox was no soldier, and as far as the evidence indicates had no military training, he was not backward in offering his recommendations for the conduct of the war in America. It seems highly probable that he offered far more advice than the records disclose. Most of his " Plans " and " Projects " are sketchily drawn. They are suggestive rather than analytical or detailed. Some of his recommendations bear witness to a high degree of consistency in policy throughout the Revolution. Others seem to be very much at variance with his mercantilistic philosophy.

The Knox and Sackville Manuscripts contain several plans in Knox's hand relative to the conduct of the war in America and its termination. Whether they were drawn up by Knox on his own initiative, or in accordance with the directions of Germain, or whether they were the product of consultations between them, is not always clear. Germain was an experienced military officer and he must have had his own ideas about the conduct of the war. The ideas of the two men so nearly coincided on most major issues that it is difficult to determine where those of Knox began and those of Germain ended. Some of these plans contain the basic ideas of policies which were consistently advocated during the Revolution.

During the early stages of the Revolution before Germain became Secretary of State, Knox submitted to Dartmouth a plan for the distribution of troops in Newfoundland, the West Indies, and Florida which suggests that he was already more concerned for the safety of the islands and the southern Colonies than for the other continental possessions.[27] On the eve of Burgoyne's departure for Canada, he proposed the organization of French Roman Catholic regiments for short term service.[28] When Burgoyne's surrender at Saratoga made French intervention fairly certain, Knox recommended a French alliance in return for the opening of the British continental Colonies in America to French trade.[29] France declared war, however, while Knox's proposition was still the subject of gossip at Spa. In October, 1778, Knox proposed to

Germain that Clinton be given permission to withdraw from Rhode Island, since its importance had been greatly diminished by the French declaration of war,[30] and directions were sent accordingly. Germain and Lord North both consulted Knox on the Penobscot expedition of 1779.[31] In the same year, and as an alternative to providing extensive reinforcements for America, he proposed to detach Spain from France by offering her West Florida and if necessary the termination of all intercourse with the Mosquito Shore.[32] He was even willing to permit Spain to control the navigation of the Mississippi in order to check expansionist tendencies in the southern Colonies.

Throughout the Revolution, the southern Colonies were one of the principal objects of Knox's concern. His preoccupation in this direction can hardly be viewed as disinterested in the light of his extensive property holdings in Georgia. As early as 1776, when he opposed the suspension of hostilities against New England, he favored a more conciliatory attitude toward the South in order to divide the Colonies and preserve a constant source of supplies for the British troops.[33] Early in August, 1777, Germain promised that as soon as news from Burgoyne arrived he would be ready to speculate with Knox about a winter campaign in the South. That he kept his promise seems evident from subsequent events and from two plans preserved in the Knox Papers.[34] Both plans are undated, but one was almost certainly drafted in the autumn of 1777 and the other before the order for the evacuation of Philadelphia in March, 1778. They contain similar proposals, based in each case on Knox's favorite assumption that the war was begun at the wrong end by attacking the " rebels " in the north where they were strongest, and where it was impossible to hold in the winter what was gained in the summer without a very considerable military force and the coöperation of the navy. On the other hand, great importance was attached to the southern Colonies which were accessible throughout the year, where the population was sparse, the Indians and the inhabitants of the back country favorably disposed to the Loyalist cause, and where the land would afford provisions for the troops and the West Indies.

Both plans presupposed the retention of Newfoundland, Nova Scotia, Canada, Bermuda, and the Bahamas. They recommended, however, that the war in the northern Colonies be confined to "a war of annoyance" maintained by incursions on New England from the Canadian frontier and raids on the sea coast to destroy "rebel" ports and shipping. The retention of New York, Rhode Island, and even Philadelphia, if there were enough Loyalists to defend it, was approved, and the seizure of a post at Penobscot advocated. Otherwise, the principal field of war operations was to be shifted to the South by concentrating reinforcements and Indian allies at St. Augustine, Augusta, and Savannah. It was proposed to send the Governor or Lieutenant-Governor of Georgia to St. Augustine to commission and mobilize the refugees and Loyalists.

In September, 1777, Germain recommended that Sir William Howe carry into execution a program similar to the one outlined above, particularly with respect to a winter campaign in the South.[35] Howe, who saw no possibility of retaining possession of the South even if it were captured, vetoed the proposition in January, 1778.[36] Nevertheless, the proposals contained in this plan continued to provide the basis for military operations during the remainder of the war. The campaign of Prevost and Campbell in Georgia during the winter of 1778 to 1779 was in line with the main project. The New Ireland plan, based on the seizure of Penobscot, was formulated in 1778 and executed as far as Penobscot was concerned in 1779.[37] Germain's secret and confidential letter to Clinton of January 23, 1779, reiterated the proposals for raids on the sea coast of the northern Colonies and for attacks on the interior from the Canadian frontier.[38] In March, 1779, James Simpson, former Attorney-General of South Carolina and member of the Assembly of that Colony, was sent to America to enlist the support of the inhabitants of the back country of Georgia and the Carolinas.³⁹ While in America, he was in constant communication with Knox.⁴⁰

The New Ireland plan, to which reference has just been made, was one of Knox's most cherished projects. In 1778, he rescued from oblivion a somewhat premature suggestion of Sir Francis Bernard in 1775 for the erection of a Loyalist colony in Maine.⁴¹ The first step in the establishment of the new colony was to be the seizure of Penobscot and the erection of a post there.⁴² Knox soon won the approval of Lord North and Germain for a scheme which fitted in well with current military plans for attacks on the rebel sea ports from Maine to New York. Instructions were sent accordingly to Clinton, who, after some delay, arranged for the seizure of Penobscot in 1779. Knox, in collaboration with Germain, then proceeded to draft a model constitution for the proposed colony, designed to eliminate the more obvious defects of the existing colonial constitutions.

The Shelburne Papers contain a draft of the plan for a new province in America between the Sawka and St. Croix Rivers, to be called New Ireland, which Knox drew up, probably as a result of his visit to Stoneland in August, and which is endorsed by Knox himself.⁴³ It is impossible to determine how much influence Germain had in its preparation. It was Knox, however, who had revived the idea of a separate government for the Eastern Provinces of Massachusetts and who had sponsored it consistently since January, 1778. Thomas Hutchinson in his *Diary* attributed the scheme entirely to him.⁴⁴ It is reasonable to assume that after more than two years' thought on the subject, Knox approached Germain with a fairly clear conception of the type of constitution he wished to establish in his model colony. The actual drafting of such a plan fell definitely within the range of his duties as Under-secretary.

The proposed constitution for New Ireland reveals only too clearly how little change four years of Revolution had effected in English official opinion on the administration of colonial possessions. Knox recommended a constitution similar to that of East Florida which would consist at the outset of a Governor and Council, a Chief Justice, and other civil officers but, for the time being, no Assembly. As a check to the republican sentiment which Knox had long deplored in the colonial Assemblies, he proposed to increase the authority of the appointive officers. Members of the Legislative Council were to be appointed by the Crown for life. To enhance the power of the Governor, Executive Councillors were to hold seats in the Legislative Council and to compose a majority there. Vacancies in the Executive Council were to be filled by members of the Legislative Council. To pave the way for a colonial aristocracy, Knox intended to bestow titles on those attached to the executive branch of the Government. The "most meritorious" Loyalists were to receive large tracts of land to be leased by them to tenants, thereby encouraging still further the development of a class system. Land grants, together with temporary exemption from the payment of quit rents, were to be provided for all Loyalists who would take an oath of allegiance to the King and Parliament. To lend additional stability to this authoritarian regime, Knox strongly advocated the establishment of the Church of England in New Ireland. Such a plan might well have satisfied the Tory elements of any community, for it paved the way for a narrow oligarchy. Indeed, the provisions of this plan bear more than a passing resemblance to the Constitutional Act of 1791 which enabled a "Family Compact" to hold sway in the Loyalist colony of Upper Canada.

In spite of the illiberal character of the model constitution, the North administration had every intention of putting it into effect. Both the plan and an estimate of £4950 for the civil establishment of the colony were approved by the Cabinet on August 10, 1780, and by the King on the following day.[45] Even the civil officers were chosen, including Peter Oliver, ex-Chief Justice of Massachusetts, for Governor.[46] On September 6, Germain informed Lieutenant-Governor Hughes of Nova Scotia that New Ireland would be established early in 1781.[47] Within the next two weeks, however, the plan struck a legal snag when Attorney-General Wedderburn raised the thorny problem of the charter rights of the people of Massachusetts. In his *Extra-Official State Papers*, Knox complained bitterly of a magistrate who was " so scrupulously observant of the sacredness of charter rights that he would not suffer them in the least to be infringed even in the case of the revolted subjects of the Massachusetts Bay." [48] The administration was unable to find an expedient to ease the troubled conscience of the Attorney-General and unwilling to risk the wrath of the House of Commons by carrying it out in the face of his opposition. The idea of establishing a Loyalist colony persisted, however, throughout the Revolution. It eventually achieved fruition in New Brunswick in 1784, largely in line with Knox's recommendations.[49]

In 1778, about the time that Knox began to urge the establishment of the Loyalist colony of New Ireland, he undertook to secure the relaxation of the commercial code with which Ireland had been saddled since the time of Charles II.[50] For at least fifteen years, Knox had expressed the conviction that Ireland must enjoy equality of status with England as far as colonial trade was concerned.[51] After 1770 his position as Under-secretary enabled him to gain the ear of influential Ministers. Lord North's reception of his objectives was so cordial that he was led to believe that once America was disposed of the Irish trade restrictions would be removed.[52] It was Germain's appointment, however, according to Knox, that insured the accomplishment of his plans. In 1776, Knox helped to secure the admission of Ireland to the southern whale fisheries.[53] In 1778, he set out to obtain the removal of at least most of the restrictions on Irish exports and imports to and from the British Colonies in America and Africa.[54]

Irish affairs were, of course, entirely outside the province of Knox as Under-secretary for American affairs. They belonged to the sphere of the Southern Department, presided over by Lord Weymouth and his secretary, Sir Stanier Porten. The official correspondence, however, is singularly barren of information respecting the relaxation of the Irish trade restrictions, especially for the year 1778, and it seems obvious that this business did not pass through the regular channels.[55] In fact, Knox, with the support of Lord North and Germain, conducted the bulk of the correspondence on this subject with the Irish administration through his letters to Sir Richard Heron, Secretary to the Lord Lieutenant, the Earl of Buckingham. Meanwhile, Knox continued to attend to his official duties in the American Department which, he says " never stood still on that account." [56] The role of Knox, unlike that of Edmund Burke, the spectacular Parliamentary orator, was essentially that of a permanent official working behind the scenes, initiating a program, preparing the minds of Ministers in both countries for its adoption, and formulating a compromise when the original plan encountered insuperable obstacles.

Owing to the bitter opposition of the English merchants, the administration was unable to achieve the sum total of its plans for the freedom of Irish trade.[57] With some important exceptions, the bill allowing Ireland to export her products to the Colonies was accepted, but the corresponding import bill was postponed. Another bill permitted Irish cotton yarn to enter England duty-free. Although these partial concessions proved of little practical importance for Ireland at the time, a very important precedent was established for the further relaxation of restrictions on Irish trade. Edmund Pery, Speaker of the Irish House of Commons, who was cognizant of the whole proceedings, credited Knox with whatever advantage Ireland derived from the trade laws of 1778.[58] Knox continued to interest himself in the Irish cause. In the same year, he helped to secure the removal of the embargo on Irish butter and beef.[59] During the following session, he conducted a successful campaign for the revision of a clause in the Fishery Act which deprived Irish fishermen of the bounties, and obtained a declaration that Irish ships were to be deemed British in all respects whatsoever.[60] Although Knox did not again assume as prominent a role as in 1778, the substance of what he had proposed for Ireland was carried into effect by February, 1780.

Among the miscellaneous and undated papers in the Sackville Manuscripts there is an anonymous document entitled "Considerations on the Great Question: What is fit to be done with America?"[61] The title and sundry corrections are unmistakably in the hand of William Knox, although the bulk of the manuscript is not. The contents, however, which include some autobiographical data and one specific reference to the writer's printed pamphlet, *The Present State of the Nation*, afford ample proof that Knox was the author. It is more difficult to establish the date of the manuscript but the contents indicate that it was drafted between 1776 and 1778, probably in the latter year, since in it Knox confidently anticipated legislation for the removal of the restrictions on Irish trade.

The "Considerations" reveals the fate mapped out for a defeated America by a Tory colonial expert. The project differs from the New Ireland Plan in that it was to be applied generally throughout the American Colonies. It indicates that Knox would not have been content with the restoration of the *status quo* in America, but was prepared to inaugurate a widespread reconstruction program to correct the capital errors of previous British colonial policy. It is significant that this memorandum was prepared for the consideration of the Cabinet and that Knox submitted copies of it to his own chief, Lord George Germain, to his former chief, Lord Dartmouth, and to the Prime Minister, Lord North.[62] It may even be the plan which met with a favorable reception from "a very intelligent cabinet."[63] Because of Knox's intimacy with his superiors, the "Considerations" may well reflect the British official mind toward the Colonies at the height of the Revolution. If so, it goes far, not only to explain the Revolution itself, but also to afford a glimpse of what might have been, or at least what might have been attempted, had Great Britain defeated the American Revolution.

To effect a complete breach with the past, Knox proposed to substitute eight provinces for the original thirteen Colonies.[64] Larger political entities, he thought, would provide greater opportunities for gradation in rank, and at the same time effectually disbar the lawless frontier element from participation in legislation, thereby leaving the government to men of property and influence. Unfortunately, Knox made no specific recommendations for the drawing of the new frontiers. He did intend to create one province in the interior along the strategic line of communication between Albany and Oswego, but whether this was to be in addition to the other eight he did not state clearly. There were to be no provinces west of the Alleghany watershed, for Knox, reverting to the principles of the Proclamation of 1763, opposed the westward expansion of America. By Act of Parliament, rather than by Proclamation, he proposed to restore the West to the Indians. There is no doubt that Knox was conscious of a frontier menace and that, like Hillsborough, he was determined to confine the Colonies to the coastal fringe of North America.

Not content with the obliteration of the old political frontiers, Knox proposed to create what he termed " a Parliamentary title " to American lands by widespread forfeiture, and the regranting of the land under conditions prescribed by Parliament. One of these conditions, to which he consistently recurred in later plans, was the compulsory subscription in future by all prospective landholders to a declaration of the supremacy of the King and Parliament over the colonies.[65] Failure to comply meant confiscation of land. Knox made special provision for the lands on the exposed communication line between Albany, Montreal, and Oswego. Here, all land was to be revested in the Crown by forfeiture, purchase, or exchange, and regranted according to the above regulations, with the additional proviso that all inhabitants do military service without pay when summoned, or else supply carriages, horses, or provisions for those who did. In return for this service, they were to be exempt by Act of Parliament from the payment of any provincial taxes, from serving on juries outside their counties, and from paying tolls on ferries and bridges. This fantastic scheme was intended to arouse the jealousy of the inhabitants of other provinces who did not enjoy these special privileges, to increase settlement in the danger zone and to encourage the colonists to look to the King and Parliament as the source of all privilege. Knox, it seems, was completely unaware of the wholesome distaste for military service so characteristic of the colonists he was trying to convert.

Knox supplemented this scheme for the defense of the frontier province with a provision for colonial disarmament throughout the rest of America which would have rendered future rebellion against Great Britain virtually impossible. He proposed to repeal all colonial militia laws, to prohibit the establishment of colonial foundries, to forbid individual Americans outside of the frontier zone to possess arms, and to transfer to the navy and to the King's troops stationed in citadels commanding great seaport towns like Boston and New York, a monopoly of colonial defense. The danger of future competition from American sea power was amply provided for by Knox by prohibiting shipyards in the colonies.

By providing for a colonial aristocracy, Knox proposed to create the social hierarchy which he found lacking in pre-Revolutionary America. He expected that its members, having a vested interest in the new regime through their control of large landed estates in the reconstructed provinces, would in time effect a real community of interest and sentiment between England and America; that the concentration of property in the hands of a few would give rise to a large tenant class, thereby subordinating the "men of mean condition" to a governing clique consisting of men of means, title, and dignity. Knox thought that a baronetage might be created at once, to be followed at the earliest feasible opportunity by a complete peerage. As it happened, this proposal to reproduce the social strata of England in frontier America never took root. The

Duke of Hudson, Viscount Pittsburgh, and Lord Potomac were not destined to control the broad acres of New York, Pennsylvania, and Maryland. The Canada Act of 1791, however, included another paper scheme for the creation of a colonial aristocracy in the Canadian provinces.

The better to counteract the prevailing tendency toward democracy in America, Knox proposed a vast increase in the powers of colonial Governors. Under the new regime, they alone were to appoint all provincial officers and clerygmen, to recommend candidates for the inferior offices in the Customs Department, and for commissions in the army. Knox, it seems, intended to provide the usual bicameral legislatures with reduced powers—a Council composed of the new aristocracy and an Assembly dominated by men of property rather than by frontiersmen. As in other instances, however, the details of his plan are conspicuous by their absence.[66] Knox did not advocate the establishment of any federal executive or legislature over the eight reconstructed colonies. Instead he reiterated the suggestion contained in *The Present State of the Nation* in favor of colonial representation in the British Parliament. In this instance he prescribed that the number of colonial delegates should be determined by American contributions to imperial defense, the maximum number for any colony being four.

To correct another capital error—failure to supply a religious hierarchy to offset the spread of republicanism—Knox recommended the establishment of the Church of England in the Colonies. Fearing the rise of an independent American church, he placed this organization entirely under the domination of the state. Clergymen, as we have seen, were to be appointed by the Governor. They were to be paid by warrant from the Crown out of a general fund raised through provincial taxation. All clergymen and teachers were expected to take the same oath of allegiance required of landholders. A dependent ecclesiastical organization could scarcely fail to inculcate Loyalist sentiments in the minds of the American colonists.

Knox devoted the rest of his memorandum to proposals designed to make the Colonies profitable. This section of the memorandum includes two suggestions for effecting a stable colonial contribution to imperial defense, one of which was of earlier origin.[67] They were intended to avoid an annual or periodic adjustment, either by Parliament or by the colonial legislatures, of the defense quota. They were both based on the premise that while Great Britain had reached the zenith of her trade and population, America was bound to increase steadily in numbers and prosperity and should, therefore, be expected to accept some form of progressive export or progressive population tax designed to support the Mother Country in old age.

Although Knox's figuring reveals some discrepancies, he had apparently made up his mind that the American Colonies should pay at least £300,000 annually toward imperial defense. Taking the population of Great Britain and her colonies as 10,000,000 and the defense budget as £4,000,000, he explained that the cost of imperial defense amounted to £40,000 for every 100,000 inhabitants. Knox proposed to charge Americans only £20,000 per 100,000 inhabitants provided they continued to pay at that rate *ad infinitum*—a program which avoided the necessity of any further consideration by Parliament or the Colonies of the annual payment. He then departed from his original estimates, or possibly made a mistake in his calculations, for he asked the two and a half million Americans to contribute £300,000, or only £12,000 per 100,000 inhabitants. Granting for the moment that such an absurd scheme could have been put into operation and that it could have continued to the present day, the United States would now be paying over $130,000,000 per annum to the defense of the British Empire! Even Grenville was never credited with such a program as this.

In his alternative program for colonial taxation, Knox set the rental of English lands against the value of American exports. For every shilling in the pound after the first two shillings assessed upon that rental, he proposed that the Americans pay a sum equal to five per cent of their exports. When, for example, the English land tax was three shillings in the pound and the value of American exports £ 3,500,000, Americans would pay £ 175,000. When the English land tax was four shillings, they would pay £ 350,000. The alleged advantage of this scheme for the Americans was that Parliament could only increase colonial taxes by first increasing English taxes. The advantage for the English, which Knox did not attempt to conceal, was that while the English land tax was likely to remain fairly constant, American taxes inevitably increased with American prosperity.[68]

The reiteration here of his plea for the restoration of Ireland to a place of equality with Great Britain in matters of colonial trade was the only liberal note sounded by Knox in the " Considerations ". In other respects, he recommended the tightening rather than the relaxation of mercantilistic bonds. Restrictions like the British monopoly of colonial trade, he regarded as merely the equivalent of benefits which accrued to the colonies, particularly their protection from foreign aggression. But Knox was no longer satisfied with this alone. He proposed to discontinue all direct trade, including that in fish, between America and Europe and even to exclude Americans from the lucrative Newfoundland fishery. In fact, he intended to cut them off as effectively as the Irish had been from the benefits of the English commercial system. Only ships owned and operated by residents of Great Britain and Ireland were to be allowed to sail the seven seas. In the Knox program there was no room for American ships or American seamen in oceanic trade. By this drastic action he expected to increase the shipping trade of the British Isles and to control American sea power.

Although Knox's brain teemed with projects designed to effect the reorganization of various parts of the empire or to increase its efficiency, this seems to have been his only general plan for the reconstruction of the American colonies. As such, it is distinctly significant, for it explains the complete failure of an influential figure in the American Department, who was regarded by the Government of the day as an expert in colonial affairs, to understand American psychology. It seems incredible that this fantastic scheme could have been deemed possible of achievement by a man who had spent five years in America. Nevertheless, as late as July, 1782, Knox entertained the possibility of his participation in a conciliation mission to effect peace with the American Colonies and fancied himself singularly fitted for the task![69] Cabinet ministers like Lord North and Germain, who confided in Knox and sought his advice, apparently shared his views or at least failed to observe their incongruity.

A study of the Under-secretary's niche in the American Department reveals the opportunity his position provided, if he were *persona grata* with his superior, of wielding an influence out of proportion to his official subordination. There is no yard stick by which that influence can be accurately measured because it depended primarily on personal relations rather than on any official status the Under-secretary may have possessed. There were seven Under-secretaries in the American Department between 1768 and 1782 but only two of them, Pownall and Knox, played a major role in the management of the office and in the determination of policy. An undue sense of modesty was not one of the principal attributes of Knox's character but there is an element of truth in his claim to have been " a principal actor in the executive government " during the American Revolution.[70] On the eve of Germain's resignation in 1782, William Eden acknowledged that whatever became of the American Department he did not see how it could exist without Knox.[71]

It is not the purpose of this study, however, to make extravagant claims with respect to the influence of the Under-secretaries in matters of colonial policy. The sole direction of colonial policy did not rest with the American Secretary, much less with his subordinates, although Hillsborough and Ger-

UNDER-SECRETARY AND COLONIAL POLICY 155

main both asserted themselves vigorously. When Sir Guy Carleton complained with particular vehemence of receiving instructions concerning military operations in Canada from Germain three thousand miles away, he was curtly informed that the major issues were not decided by him alone but received the fullest consideration from the Cabinet and the approval of the King before their adoption.[72] Even when the Cabinet agreed to a particular line of conduct, George III sometimes balked the execution of their designs.

1 See chap. iii, p. 37.
2 Dartmouth MSS, Box 11, No. 448, "A Londoner" to Dartmouth, October, 1772.
3 Smyth, *Franklin*, V, 446, Benjamin Franklin to William Franklin, November 3, 1772.
4 [Almon], *Biographical, Literary and Political Anecdotes*, II, 112.
5 Knox Papers, X, 21, Proceedings in relation to the American Colonies. Knox says elsewhere that he enjoyed the complete confidence of Hillsborough, Dartmouth and Germain. See Knox, *Extra-Official State Papers*, I, 26.
6 See, for example, Dartmouth MSS, Nos. 898, 1500, 1514.
7 *Ibid.*, No. 1485, Pownall to Dartmouth, September 5, 1775.
8 *Ibid.*, No. 1514, Pownall to Dartmouth, September 12, 1775.
9 Knox, *Extra-Official State Papers*, I, 5.
10 Knox Papers, X, 31, Removal of Lord George Germain. Knox himself claimed that their relationship was one of "fervent friendship" and that Germain had "unbounded confidence" in him. Knox, *Extra-Official State Papers*, I, Appendix III, p. 8.
11 For further discussion, see chap. v.
12 Knox, *Extra-Official State Papers*, II, 43-4.
13 Knox Papers, X, 21, Proceedings in relation to the American Colonies.
14 *Ibid.*
15 Dartmouth MSS, Box 13, No. 520, Pownall to Dartmouth, January 4, 1773.
16 *Ibid.*, No. 871, Pownall to Dartmouth, August 5, 1773.
17 *Ibid.*, No. 886, Pownall to Dartmouth, October 6, 1773; *ibid.*, No. 887, Knox to Dartmouth, October 6, 1773.
18 *Ibid.*, No. 1427, Pownall to Dartmouth, August 5, 1775; *ibid.*, No. 1424, Knox to Dartmouth, August 5, 1775.
19 Knox Papers, X, 21.
20 *Ibid.*, II, 21, Knox to Blackburn, February 15, 1775.
21 *Ibid.*, I, 27, Grenville to Knox, June 27, 1768; *ibid.*, 30, Grenville to Knox, July 15, 1768.

22 *Ibid.*, II, 21, Knox to Blackburn, February 15, 1775.
23 Compare this scheme with the Nova Scotian loyal address of June 24, 1775, discussed by J. B. Brebner in "Nova Scotia's Remedy for the American Revolution," *Canadian Historical Review*, XV, 171-81 (June, 1934). There seems to be no evidence to suggest that the Knox proposal of February, 1775, produced the Nova Scotian response in June, 1775, or the Nova Scotian Bill of June, 1776, which levied an eight per cent duty on all foreign imports except Bay salt. On the other hand, the address, which recommended that the proportion of colonial payments be fixed in such a way as to avoid annual or periodic adjustments, and which at the same time proposed a tax which would increase with colonial prosperity, bears a striking resemblance to a later Knox proposal of 1778 (?). See *infra*, p. 152. Knox was not in the habit of acknowledging the source of the various projects which he adopted and claimed as his own.
24 *Parliamentary History*, XVIII, 333.
25 *Knox Papers*, I, 30.
26 *Ibid.*, IX, 23, Project of a Permanent Union and Settlement with the Colonies.
27 *Ibid.*, IX, 18, Idea of a Plan for carrying on the war (Endorsed, 1775).
28 *Ibid.*, 16 and 17 (2 drafts), Plan for raising soldiers in Canada.
29 *Ibid.*, VII, 26.
30 *Ibid.*, IV, 39, Knox to Germain, October 31, 1778.
31 See *infra*, p. 144.
32 Knox Papers, IX, 28, Peace or War.
33 *Ibid.*, X, 23, The First Commissioners to the American Colonies.
34 *Ibid.*, IX, 21 and 22.
35 C. O. 5, Vol. 94, pp. 610-02, Germain to Howe, No. 19, September 3, 1777.
36 *Ibid.*, Vol. 236, Howe to Germain, January 16, 1778.
37 See *infra*, p. 144.
38 C. O. 5, Vol. 97, pp. 25 *et seq.*, Germain to Clinton (Secret & Confidential), January 23, 1779.
39 *Ibid.*, p. 295, Germain to Clinton, March 31, 1779, introducing Simpson.
40 See chap. vi, notes 32 and 41.
41 Dartmouth MSS, Box 28, No. 1223, Bernard to Dartmouth, April 18, 1775.
42 There is an extensive bibliography on New Ireland. It will suffice to mention here, Marion Gilroy, "The Partition of Nova Scotia," *Canadian Historical Review*, XIV, 375 (December, 1933); *ibid.*, XVI, 91 (March, 1935); J. B. Brebner, "The Partition of Nova Scotia," *ibid.*, XV (March, 1934); J. B. Brebner, *The Neutral Yankees of Nova Scotia* (New York, 1937), pp. 329-30; [John Calef], *The Siege of Penobscot by the Rebels* . . . (London, 1781); S. F. Batchelder, *The Life and Surprising Adventures of John Nutting* . . . (Reprinted from the *Proceedings of the Cambridge Historical Society*, Cambridge, 1912). Nutting, who had a saw-mill at Penobscot, first converted Knox, and at his request wrote to Germain to urge the seizure of the post. See C. O. 5, Vol. 155, No. 88, John Nutting to Germain, January 17, 1778.

## UNDER-SECRETARY AND COLONIAL POLICY 157

43 Shelburne MSS, Vol. 66, pp. 513-28, "Proposal for making a new province in America to be called New Ireland &c, with an estimate of the Civil Establishment for that Province." Endorsed: "Approved by the King, 11 August, 1780."

44 Hutchinson, *Diary*, II, 290, October 20, 1779.

45 Shelburne MSS, Vol. 66, p. 513; also Knox Papers, V, 44.

46 *Ibid.*; *ibid.*, 45; C. O. 5, Vol. 175, Peter Oliver to Knox, August 19, 1780.

47 C. O. 217, Vol. 55, p. 238, Germain to Hughes, September 6, 1780.

48 Knox, *Extra-Official State Papers*, II, 60.

49 The writer expects to publish a more extensive account of the New Ireland Plan at some future date. See Knox, *Extra-Official State Papers*, II, Appendix XIV, pp. 47-54, for Knox's plan to partition Nova Scotia; also C. O. 217, Vol. 56, pp. 408 ff. for another draft of the same.

50 The Navigation Act of 1663 first restrained Irish trade by preventing Irish ships from carrying European products to the colonies. It also deprived Irish ships of the right to transport fish to England. An Act of 1670 confirmed the exclusion of Ireland from the colonial trade and another of 1696 terminated the direct importation of enumerated commodities from the English Colonies into England. Similar Acts prohibited the export of leading Irish products into England.

51 Knox Papers, IX, 4, " Hints relative to our Commerce " (1763 ?); Knox, *The Present State of the Nation* (London, 1768), p. 70.

52 Knox, *Extra-Official State Papers*, I, 4.

53 *Ibid.*, Appendixes II and III.

54 Knox has published his correspondence on this subject in his *Extra-Official State Papers*, Vol. I.

55 See, for example, the State Papers Domestic, Ireland, S. P. 63, Vols. 459-60. The official correspondence deals almost entirely with matters relative to military commissions and appointments, and to the measures for the relief of Roman Catholics. In Volume 460, p. 64, there is a letter from Heron to Porten, May 10, 1778, transmitting a copy of a letter he has sent to Knox. On the other hand, for the year 1779 this series contains valuable information regarding the trade concessions. There was some correspondence between Buckingham and North on these measures, but unfortunately the North Papers of this period seem to have disappeared. Copies of a few of Buckingham's letters to North were sent to Knox.

56 Knox, *Extra-Official State Papers*, I, Part 2, note opposite p. 14.

57 *Journals of the House of Commons*, XXXVI, 938-960. *Ibid.*, Appendix 24.

58 Knox, *Extra-Official State Papers*, I, Appendix XLI, Pery to Knox, August 6, 1778.

59 *Ibid.*, p. 9; *ibid.*, Appendix XLII, O'Brien to Knox, September 20, 1778. Sir Lucius O'Brien gives Knox a large measure of credit for securing the removal of the embargo on Irish butter. See also Knox Papers, XI, 54, " Papers delivered to Lord G. G. which procured the Revocation of the Embargo on Irish Provisions, December, 1778."

60 *Statutes at Large*, IX, pp. 73-5, for the act of 20 Geo. III, cap. 10.

**61** Sackville MSS, Miscellaneous and Undated.

**62** In submitting his copy to Dartmouth, Knox said that he had given one to Lord North "which it is hoped will overturn all his ideas of patching up matters with the colonies." See *Hist. MSS Comm., Dartmouth MSS*, II, 451. When the author examined the originals at Patshull House, this document was missing or had been misplaced.

**63** Knox, *Extra-Official State Papers*, I, Appendix V, p. 74.

**64** It is possible that Knox was consciously or unconsciously under the influence of Sir Francis Bernard, an ardent advocate of the proposed Loyalist colony of New Ireland, who favored consolidation of the thirteen colonies into a few large provinces. See *Select Letters on the Government of America and the Principles of Law and Polity Applied to the American Colonies* (London, 1774), written in 1764. However, Knox makes no reference here to Bernard's work.

**65** Dartmouth MSS, No. 331, "Thoughts upon the Reform of the Constitution of the Massachusetts Bay" [1770].

**66** The form of government is suggested here rather than clearly outlined, but in other instances Knox favored the usual model of Governor, Council, and at least eventually, an Assembly, being satisfied to shift the balance of power to the executive and appointive officials.

**67** Knox Papers, IX, 23, "Project of a Permanent Union and Settlement with the Colonies."

**68** *Cf. supra*, p. 156 n. 23.

**69** Sackville MSS, America and Miscellaneous, 1774-1782, Knox to Sackville, July 6, 1782.

**70** Knox, *Extra-Official State Papers*, II, 3-4.

**71** Knox Papers, XI, 66, Wm. Eden to Knox, February 11, 1782.

**72** *Ibid.*, III, 19, Germain to [Carleton], July 10, 1777.

# CHAPTER X
# THE ABOLITION OF THE AMERICAN DEPARTMENT

SINCE the Colonial Department had assumed the major responsibility for the direction of the American War, it naturally bore the brunt of military defeat. Yorktown provided the opponents of Lord North and the King's system with the opportunity for which they had long been looking—a first-class excuse to discredit the Government. An American Department without the American Colonies would, of course, have been an anomaly. But the American Department was not judged according to its own merits or demerits. In the minds of the leaders of the Whig Opposition it had to go, largely because it stood as a symbol of the system which they were determined to destroy and an important element in it.

The position of the Opposition was revealed clearly enough even before the surrender of Cornwallis. In February, 1780, Edmund Burke introduced a Bill for Economical Reform which contemplated, among other changes, the suppression of the American Department.[1] His avowed objectives were twofold, namely, economy and the diminution of the influence of the Crown. Since the King maintained his power by a judicious dispensation of places and pensions among his supporters, Burke's objectives were intimately related. By a drastic reduction in the cost of Government, he hoped to effect his second aim, the overthrow of the King's influence. According to his own estimate, he expected to save £10,000 per year on the American Department alone.[2]

Burke's arguments in favor of the abolition of the Third Secretaryship were singularly lacking in statesmanship and in understanding of the problem of colonial administration. His assertions that the department was a sinecure, that its uselessness was notorious, and that its correspondence was trifling in quantity, were gross exaggerations. The fact that Weymouth had been able to administer the Northern and Southern Departments for a period of several months following Suffolk's death was no sound basis for Burke's conclusion that if one Secretary could do the work of two, two would be equal to the work of three. This was not the opinion of the Duke of Grafton in 1767 when he assured Shelburne that not even a Solomon could manage the affairs of the Southern Department satisfactorily.[3] Burke's inference was patently unfair. The American War had easily doubled the work of the Colonial Office, whereas, if anything, it actually reduced the labors of the other two Secretaries.

The clumsy and illogical division of foreign affairs between the two " ancient " Secretaries did not deter Burke from recommending a similar division of colonial business. He proposed to return the management of the Colonies to either of the other Secretaries or better still, to divide it between them, giving North America to the Northern and the West Indies to the Southern Secretary. George III recommended a more sensible division of labor among the Secretaries in 1770 when he proposed to maintain the Colonial Department, to give the entire conduct of foreign affairs to Lord Rochford, and domestic affairs, including Scotland and Ireland, to Suffolk.[4] It can only be said that Burke at the time showed more enthusiasm for economy and for the reduction of the King's influence than for efficiency in colonial administration. Thomas Townshend was equally unaware of the possibilities of a well organized Colonial Department when he argued that the country which had raised itself to the pitch of national glory under two Secretaries of State, and which had been reduced to ruin and disgrace by the appointment of a third, should therefore return to its former system of management.[5]

There seems to have been a complete absence of any investigation into the management of the Colonial Office prior to the demand for its abolition. Fox, who shared Burke's opinion that the department was a cog in the King's system, regarded its uselessness as so obvious that it required no further investigation.⁶ It is true that the various branches of Government were compelled to submit reports to the House of Commons in May, 1780, but the information contained in these were limited to figures on the number employed, their salaries, and the general expenses of the department concerned.⁷ This information hardly afforded sufficient evidence of the uselessness of any of the other departments affected by Burke's Bill. Whether the members of the staff of the American Office were invited to testify before the House is not entirely clear. That this may have been done is implied in Burke's assertion that neither the deputy, the clerks, nor even the fire-lighter would come to vouch for the department.⁸ Burke, however, refused to ask John Pownall to speak for the Board of Trade on the ground that one who had made his fortune out of the office would scarcely present an unbiassed opinion.⁹ It would have been interesting and perhaps enlightening to have had Burke and Knox, who had already matched wits as pamphleteers in 1768, debate the issues at stake in 1780.

The defense of the American Department in the House of Commons was weak and ineffective. Lord Beauchamp made a dull and unconvincing speech on behalf of the King's system. Charles Jenkinson, without bothering to list his reasons, claimed that the department was useful and that the King's influence was already declining. Germain, who was present during the debate and who might have been expected to defend his own office, seems to have been more interested in having his title, as " one of His Majesty's principal Secretaries," correctly stated in the Bill.¹⁰ It would appear that the King's Friends were still sufficiently certain of their majority to feel it unnecessary to exert themselves unduly against the Opposition. If so, their optimism was scarcely justified. The vote came at two forty-five A. M. in the Committee of the House with 201 for the Bill and 208 against it. For the time being, the American Department was saved by the narrow margin of seven votes. The debate of 1780 nevertheless foreshadowed the end. The next step in that direction was the resignation of Germain.

The news of the surrender of Cornwallis at Yorktown in October, 1781, which destroyed all hope of success against America for the time being, if not permanently, was the prelude to the resignation of Germain. Led by Richard Rigby and Henry Dundas,[11] the Opposition Whigs took advantage of the consequent discontent over the conduct of the American War to attempt the overthrow of the North administration. The first "human sacrifice" Dundas demanded was Germain.[12] His removal, predicted by Thomas Pownall as early as November 29, 1781,[13] was to be followed by attacks on Sandwich, the head of the Admiralty, and finally on Lord North himself.

Almost inevitably the approach of Germain's departure revived the idea of abolishing his department. George III had it in mind at the end of 1781 when he recommended that Lord Stormont take over the entire conduct of foreign affairs and that Hillsborough manage domestic business and the Colonies.[14] In January, 1782, the rumor that the office was not to be filled, since its province was gone, reached the ears of Horace Walpole.[15] Although the King betrayed a very human tendency to blame the department for the embarrassing predicament in which he found himself, he did not surrender it without a struggle. Apparently, he expected to save the North Administration by reorganization of the Cabinet and the sacrifice of Germain. That he made a real effort to save the American Department seems evident from his diligent search for another Colonial Secretary and his satisfaction over the ultimate appointment of Welbore Ellis. But the tide of events proved too strong for him. Crushing military defeat in America had directed the attacks of the Opposition against the department responsible for the conduct of the war, the department which was at the same time so closely associated in men's minds with the triumph of the King's system.

Germain's position was wide open to attack after Yorktown. Even the King had ceased to regard him as a useful person in his department, although he still subscribed wholeheartedly to Germain's unflinching opposition to the surrender of the Colonies.[16] Lord North and Germain had not been on good terms since 1778 when the Prime Minister failed to consult his American Secretary about his appeasement program of sending peace commissioners to the Colonies.[17] Lord North was undoubtedly embarrassed by attacks in the House of Commons and felt that some concessions to the Opposition would be necessary to save the administration. He was aware, however, that his enemies would not be content with the mere dismissal of Germain, since they objected more to the system than to the Secretary. Moreover, he found Germain very useful in the House of Commons where, he informed the King, his position would be intolerable "if there should be no Minister there acquainted with American affairs, and ready to answer these points when they occur, as they do almost every day in debate."[18] The Prime Minister would have been relieved if Germain had released him from an embarrassing predicament by resigning on his own initiative, but this the American Secretary refused to do. He would retire only if the King and the Prime Minister requested him to do so in the best interests of the nation. In December, Germain was apparently seeking an honorable way out, but he was loath to give the impression of running away from a dangerous and disagreeable situation.[19]

For the first six weeks of 1782 a state of indecision prevailed as to the fate of Germain and his department. Meanwhile, business in the Colonial Office was at a standstill and preparations for the 1782 campaign were hopelessly delayed. According to Knox, Germain avoided Cabinet meetings and spent most of his time out of town.[20] Even the King became annoyed at the way in which Germain was kept "dangling" for weeks because of Lord North's dilatory tactics in seeking a successor.[21] It was not a simple matter to find a successor who would agree to take over a discredited office in a tottering administration in time of defeat. Charles Jenkinson, to whom it was offered, refused pointblank to have any dealings with a Prime Minister as indecisive as Lord North.[22] Apparently without consulting his Cabinet,[23] but with the consent of the King, Lord North then offered the post to Welbore Ellis, a veteran placeman of no particular talent, who could scarcely have been expected to direct Colonial policy for any length of time. Knox, who knew of the proposed change as early as February 1, notified William Eden, who was with Lord Carlisle in Ireland, that if Ellis refused the appointment the office would merge for the time being with the Southern Department.[24] By his acceptance, Ellis postponed the change for approximately a month.[25] Meanwhile the resignation of Germain was interpreted rightly or wrongly as the abandonment of plans for the suppression of rebellion in the colonies.[26]

With the fall of Lord North in March, 1782, the position of Third Secretary was permitted to lapse. Rockingham appointed only two principal Secretaries, Fox and Shelburne, the latter in accordance with the King's plan retaining the Southern Department and the Colonies, while Fox assumed the entire conduct of foreign affairs. Shelburne, who had bitterly resented the establishment of the Colonial Department in 1768, must have considered this arrangement a just retribution. Despite the lack of positive evidence, it seems likely that in 1782 he used whatever influence he had to prevent the appointment of a Third Secretary. No order-in-council recorded this new division of labor among the Secretaries. Fox announced the change to the British representatives abroad in a circular letter, as follows:

The King having on the resignation of the Lord Viscount Stormont, been pleased to appoint me one of His Principal Secretaries of State and at the same time to make a new arrangement in the Departments by conferring that for Domestic Affairs and Colonies on the Earl of Shelburne, and entrusting me with the sole direction of the Department of Foreign Affairs, I am to desire you will for the future address your letters to me.[27]

ABOLITION OF THE AMERICAN DEPARTMENT 165

The change thus formally introduced seems to have called forth even less comment than the establishment of the Third Secretaryship in 1768. *The Annual Register* did not devote a sentence to the event and even the redoubtable Horace Walpole passed it over in silence. The Act of 22 George III, cap. 82 formally abolished the office " commonly called or known by the name of Third Secretary of State, or Secretary of State for the Colonies " and expressly declared that any similar office hereafter established must be considered a new office.[28] The Board of Trade shared the same fate, its business being transferred to a committee of the Privy Council.

In spite of Burke's clamor for economy, adequate compensation was given to the members of the Colonial Office staff whose positions were suppressed.[29] An exception was made in the case of William Knox whose pension from the King of £ 1200 per annum was already greatly in excess of that usually granted to Under-secretaries of State. John Fisher, however, who had been connected with the department for only six months, received an annuity of £ 400. All in all, annuities worth £ 2,050 were distributed among the members of the Colonial Office, in comparison with £ 2,275 awarded to the Board of Trade. Only three members of the staff were transferred to the Home Office, namely, the veteran chief clerk, William Pollock, and two ordinary clerks, Eardley Wilmot and George Palman. Shelburne intended to collect in his own department the most capable members of the three offices, the Board of Trade, the Colonial Office, and the Southern Department.[30] With this end in view, he commissioned Grey Elliott, the Clerk of Reports in the Board of Trade, to draw up a suitable plan. Before this could be accomplished, however, the administration changed hands, and no more was heard of the scheme.

In conclusion, it may be said that the American Department had a stormy history during its fourteen years of existence. From 1768 to 1775 its prerogative was constantly challenged by the other two Secretaries and for the rest of the period it had to function under abnormal circumstances. Undoubtedly, it served a useful purpose in correlating the work of various branches of the Government concerned with colonial business. It was a step in the right direction, but its successful operation would have necessitated a political and administrative housecleaning in all the major offices. The department was too closely associated with George III's entrenchment in power to be regarded with anything but suspicion by the more liberal imperialists of the day, including Burke and Fox. It was therefore logical that its abolition should coincide with a powerful, if not entirely successful, attack on the King's system.

Lord Chesterfield's prediction in 1766 that the creation of an American Department might save America was not fulfilled in practice. Because the Revolution terminated in the loss of the Thirteen Colonies, the department has been deemed a failure. It seems unlikely, however, that under the previous administration of colonial affairs by the Southern Department, the situation would have been any better or the results different. In fact, the return of the colonies to the Southern or Home Office in 1782 was accompanied by no major change in policy toward the remaining British colonies. It is perhaps safe to say that the creation of the American Department had a more direct effect upon English politics than upon colonial policy. If anything, its establishment more firmly entrenched the policy of coercion, the signs of which were evident even in the many so-called conciliatory proposals of the administration. Under these circumstances, it is likewise doubtful if a more liberal personnel, including a Franklin, would have had any greater influence than Dartmouth in modifying the attitude of the King's Friends. Even if the department had been granted the full and undisputed powers called for by Chesterfield, it is difficult to believe that the personnel in control would have made any drastic changes in colonial or military policies. The history of the American Department and its relations with the other branches of administration afford a very clear illustration of the fact that in the Revolutionary War the English Government kept on muddling, but definitely failed to "muddle through."

## ABOLITION OF THE AMERICAN DEPARTMENT 167

1 *Parliamentary History*, XXI, 54 *et seq.*, 193 ff.
2 Burke, *Correspondence* (London, 1844), II, 325.
3 See *supra*, p. 19.
4 *Correspondence of George III*, II, no. 882, pp. 205-06, King to North, January 13, 1771.
5 *Parliamentary History*, XXI, 199.
6 *Ibid.*, p. 152.
7 See chap. iii, note 4.
8 *Parliamentary History*, XXI, 154.
9 *Ibid.*, p. 239.
10 *Ibid.*, p. 193.
11 Knox Papers, X, 31, Removal of Lord George Germain.
12 *Correspondence of George III*, V, No. 3511, p. 359, Jenkinson to the King, February 3, 1782; also Stevens's *Facsimiles*, X, 1051, Knox to [Wm. Eden], February 1, 1782.
13 Brit. Mus., Add. MSS, 20733, Almon Correspondence, November 29, 1781.
14 *Correspondence of George III*, V, no. 3485, p. 326, King to North, December 26, 1781.
15 Walpole, *Letters*, XII, 148, Walpole to Sir Horace Mann, January 18, 1782.
16 *Correspondence of George III*, IV, Nos. 2202, 2510, 2626, 2657; *ibid.*, V, No. 3501, p. 334.
17 See *supra*, p. 75.
18 *Correspondence of George III*, V, 335-7, Lord North to the King [January 21, 1782].
19 Sackville MSS, Letters to Genl. Irwin, 1761-84, Germain to Irwin, December 22, 1781.
20 Knox, *Extra-Official State Papers*, I, 44.
21 *Correspondence of George III*, V, 334, King to North, January 21, 1782.
22 *Ibid.*, p. 338, Jenkinson to the King, January 22, 1782.
23 Brit. Mus., Add. MSS, 34418, f. 323, Ed. Smith to William Eden, February 8, 1782. Smith reports that no one in the Cabinet knew that Ellis had been selected to succeed Germain until February 7, 1782, and that "some resent it gruffly."
24 Stevens's *Facsimiles*, X, 1051, Knox to [Wm. Eden], February 1, 1782.
25 Welbore Ellis received the Seals on February 11, 1782, and resigned on March 27, 1782.
26 Walpole, *Letters*, XII, 149, Walpole to the Countess of Upper Ossory, January 19, 1782; see also, D. M. Clark, *British Opinion and the American Revolution* (New Haven, 1930), p. 251.
27 Quoted, Anson, *Law and Custom of the Constitution* (4th rev. ed., Oxford and N. Y., 1909), II, pt. 1, pp. 165-66.
28 *Statutes at Large*, XIV, 262. The other offices abolished at the same time were as follows: the Board of Trade, the offices of the Lords of Police in Scotland, the principal Officers of the Board of Ordnance, the Great Ward-

robe, the Jewel Office, the office of Treasurer of the Chamber, the office of Cofferer of the Household, the Board of Green Cloth, Paymaster of the Pensions, Master of the Harriers and Fox Hounds, and the Master of the Stag Hounds.

29 Treasury Papers, T 1, Vol. 338, p. 174, " List of Compensations granted to Persons whose Offices have been suppressed." The following is an abstract of the amount granted to each department:

| | |
|---|---|
| Lord Chamberlain's Office | £2036 |
| Lord Steward's Office | 1341 |
| Master of the Horse | 1335 |
| Office of Robes | 525 |
| Housekeepers | 1050 |
| Office of Police | 600 |
| Great Wardrobe | 640 |
| Removing Wardrobe | 390 |
| Paymaster of Pensions | 220 |
| Secretary of State | 2050 |
| Cofferer's Office | 320 |
| Board of Trade | 2275 |
| Board of Works | 1118 |
| Jewel Office | 240 |
| Treasurer of the Chamber's Office | 250 |
| Total | £14,390 |

30 Knox Papers, X, 35, Marquis of Lansdowne.

# BIBLIOGRAPHY

## MANUSCRIPT SOURCES

*Departmental Correspondence*

The official correspondence of the various departments of the British Government between 1768 and 1782 is to be found in the Public Record Office. The COLONIAL OFFICE PAPERS for these years represent the bulk of the author's research in the official correspondence. The AUDIT OFFICE PAPERS, Series 12 and 13, contain the petitions of Loyalists like William Knox and John Fisher, Under-secretaries of the American Department. The BOARD OF WORKS PAPERS were examined only for references to the location of the offices of the American Department. The STATE PAPERS DOMESTIC were used for the relaxation of restrictions on Irish trade, 1778-1779. STATE PAPERS DOMESTIC, VARIOUS, Vol. 32, contains the Colonial Office Fee Book. The papers of the other branches of the administration were consulted chiefly with reference to inter-departmental correspondence.

ADMIRALTY PAPERS. In Letters, Out Letters, 1768-1782.

AUDIT OFFICE PAPERS, Series 12 and 13. Loyalist Claims.

BOARD OF TRADE PAPERS, 1768-1782.

BOARD OF WORKS PAPERS, 1768, 1782.

COLONIAL OFFICE PAPERS, 1768-1782.

PATENT ROLLS, 1768-1782.

PRIVY COUNCIL PAPERS, 1768-1782. Committee Reports; Register.

STATE PAPERS DOMESTIC, IRELAND, Vols. 459-465.

STATE PAPERS DOMESTIC, VARIOUS, Vol. 32, The Colonial Office Fee Book.

TREASURY PAPERS, 1768-1782. Minutes, In Letters, Out Letters, Law Opinions, Reports of the Commissioners of Accounts, Papers on Ireland.

WAR OFFICE PAPERS, 1768-1782.

KNOX PAPERS, 1756-1810 (11 Vols.). The William L. Clements Library, Ann Arbor, Michigan. This collection contains the bulk of what remains of William Knox's correspondence with his superiors and friends during this period, together with many papers on miscellaneous subjects. Calendar: *Hist. MSS Comm., Various Coll.*, Vol. VI (London, 1909).

PRIVATE PAPERS OF WILLIAM KNOX. These include a small collection of personal letters and papers, many undated, which are now in the possession of Captain H. V. Knox of Oxford. Their importance is chiefly biographical.

DARTMOUTH MANUSCRIPTS, 1763-1783 (Patshull House). The papers of William Legge, second Earl of Dartmouth. Only those relating to Dartmouth's term as Colonial Secretary, 1772-1775, to his correspondence with John Pownall and William Knox, were examined. Calendar: *Hist. MSS Comm.*, 11th, 14th and 15th *Reports* (London, 1887, 1895, 1896).

DARTMOUTH MANUSCRIPTS, 1757-1776 (Canadian Archives). Letters and Papers relating to Canada.

SACKVILLE MANUSCRIPTS, 1775-1783. These papers, which contain the bulk of the correspondence of Lord George Germain, Viscount Sackville, Secretary of State for the Colonies, 1775-1782, were examined at the home of the late William L. Clements in Bay City, Michigan. They include William Knox's remarkable project for the reconstruction of the empire. Calendar: *Hist. MSS Comm.* (2 vols., London, 1904).

SACKVILLE MANUSCRIPTS, 1775-1783 (Drayton). These papers are now the property of Captain Nigel Victor Stopford-Sackville. Those examined referred to Ireland.

SHELBURNE MANUSCRIPTS, 1760-1783. The papers of William Petty Fitzmaurice, Earl of Shelburne and Marquess of Lansdowne. Both the originals in the William L. Clements Library and the transcripts in the Canadian Archives were consulted.

ADDITIONAL MANUSCRIPTS IN THE BRITISH MUSEUM

> AUCKLAND PAPERS, 1772-1784. The correspondence and papers of William Eden, first Baron Auckland, Under-secretary in the Northern Department, 1772-1778, member of the Board of Trade, 1776-1782, and one of the Peace Commissioners sent to America in 1778.
>
> HALDIMAND PAPERS, 1778-1782. The papers of General Sir Frederick Haldimand, Governor of Canada. The transcripts in the Canadian Archives were used, with occasional reference, where necessary, to the originals in the British Museum.
>
> NEWCASTLE PAPERS, 1751-1768. The official correspondence of Thomas Pelham Holles, Duke of Newcastle, 1697-1768. For the origin of the American Department.

CHATHAM PAPERS, Bundles 101-363, Public Record Office. Only the second series, the papers of William Pitt the Younger, were examined.

RODNEY PAPERS. The correspondence of Admiral George Brydges Rodney, 1719-1792. Public Record Office. Volume 15 contains a printed statement of the case of William Knox for compensation as a Loyalist.

STOWE MANUSCRIPTS. British Museum. Vol. 163, ff. 168-9, " Table of Fees in the Secretary of State's Office."

## PRINTED SOURCES

*Documents, Debates*

*Acts and Resolves, Public and Private, of the Province of Massachusetts Bay* (Boston, 1869-1922).

Candler, Allen D. (ed.), *The Colonial Records of the State of Georgia* (Atlanta, Georgia, 1907).

Cobbett's *Parliamentary History of England* (London, 1806-1820).

Force, Peter (ed.), *American Archives* (Washington, 1837-53).

Ford, W. C. (ed.), *Journals of the Continental Congress, 1774-1789* (Washington, 1904-36).

BIBLIOGRAPHY 171

Great Britain, *Statutes at Large* (London, 1763-1800).
——, *Journals of the House of Commons* (London, 1803).
Munro, James and Fitzroy, Sir Almeric W. (eds.), *Acts of the Privy Council of England, Colonial Series*, Vols. V and VI (H. M. Stationery Office, London, 1912).
*Reports from Committees of the House of Commons, 1715-1801* (London, 1803-1806).
*Reports of the Historical Manuscripts Commission* on the MSS of the Earl of Dartmouth, Mrs. Stopford Sackville, J. B. Fortescue, Lord Emly, Captain H. V. Knox, Mar and Kellie, the American Manuscripts in the Royal Institution of Great Britain, and the Abergavenny MSS (London, various dates).
Stevens, B. F. (ed.), *Facsimiles of Documents in European Archives Relating to America, 1773-1783* (London, 1891).

*Contemporary Pamphlets*

[Anon.], *The First Measures Necessary to be taken in the American Department* (London, 1768).
Bateson, Mary (ed.), *A Narrative of the Changes in the Ministry, 1765-1767. Told by the Duke of Newcastle in a series of Letters to John White, M.P.* (London, 1898).
[Burke, Edmund], *Observations on a Late State of the Nation* (Dublin, 1769).
J. C., Esq. [John Calef], *The Siege of Penobscot by the Rebels &c.* (London, 1871; New York, reprinted, 1910).
[Knox, Wm.], *The Claim of the Colonies to an Exemption from Internal Taxes imposed by Authority of Parliament, Examined* (London, 1765).
——, *A Letter to a Member of Parliament wherein the Power of the British Legislature, and the Case of the Colonists, are briefly and impartially Considered* (London, 1765).
——, *The Present State of the Nation* (Dublin, 1768).
——, *An Appendix to the Present State of the Nation Containing a Reply to the Observations on the Pamphlet* (London, 1769).
——, *The Controversy Between Great Britain and her Colonies Reviewed* (London, 1769).
——, *The Interest of the Merchants and Manufacturers of Great Britain, in the Present Contest with the Colonies, Stated and Considered* (London, 1774).
——, *The Justice and Policy of the Late Act of Parliament for Making More Effectual Provision for the Government of the Province of Quebec, Asserted and Proved* (London, 1774; New York, 1774).
——, *Considerations on the State of Ireland* (Dublin, 1778).
——, *Extra-Official State Papers* (2 vols., London, 1789).
[Pownall, Thomas], *The Administration of the Colonies* (London, 1764).

*Correspondence, Memoirs, and Diaries*

Albemarle, George Thomas, Earl of (ed.), *Memoirs of the Marquis of Rockingham and his Contemporaries* (London, 1852).

# BIBLIOGRAPHY

Anson, Sir William R. (ed.), *Autobiography and Political Correspondence of Augustus Henry Third Duke of Grafton* (London, 1898).
Barnes, G. R. and Owen, J. H. (eds.), *The Private Papers of John, Earl of Sandwich, First Lord of the Admiralty, 1771-1782* (4 vols., London, 1932-38).
"Bowdoin and Temple Papers," *Massachusetts Historical Society Collections*, 6th Series, Vol. IX (Boston, 1897).
Channing, Edward and Coolidge, A. C., *The Barrington-Bernard Correspondence and Illustrative Matter, 1760-1770* (Cambridge, 1912).
Donne, W. B., *Correspondence of George the Third with Lord North from 1768 to 1783* (2 vols., London, 1867).
Fitzwilliam, Charles Wm., Earl, and Bourke, Lieut. Gen. Sir Richard (eds.), *Correspondence of Edmund Burke, 1744-1797* (London, 1844).
Flanders, Henry (ed.), *Memoirs of Richard Cumberland* (Philadelphia, 1856).
Fortescue, J. B. (ed.), *The Correspondence of George III* (London, 1927-8).
Franklin, Wm. Temple (ed.), *Memoirs of the Life and Writings of Benjamin Franklin* (3 vols., London, 1818).
Hutchinson, P. O. (ed.), *The Diary and Letters of His Excellency Thomas Hutchinson* (London, 1883-6).
"Letters of the Hon. James Habersham, 1756-1775," *Collections of the Georgia Historical Society*, Vol. VI (Savannah, 1904).
Penruddocke, Henry (ed.), *The Diary of the Late George Bubb Dodington, Baron of Melcombe Regis, From March 8, 1749 to February 6, 1761* (Salisbury, 1784).
Raymond, Rev. W. O. (ed.), *Winslow Papers, 1776-1826* (St. John, N. B., 1901).
Sheffield, Lord John (ed.), *The Miscellaneous Works of Edward Gibbon*, Vol. I, "Memoirs and Letters" (London, 1814).
Smith, Wm. Jas. (ed.), *Grenville Papers* (4 vols., London, 1853).
Smyth, Albert H. (ed.), *The Writings of Benjamin Franklin* (10 vols., New York, 1905-07).
Taylor, W. S. and Pringle, J. H. (eds.), *Chatham Correspondence* (4 vols., London, 1838).
Toynbee, Mrs. Paget (ed.), *The Letters of Horace Walpole* (Oxford, 1903-5).
"Trumbull Papers," *Massachusetts Historical Society Collections*, 5th Series, Vol. IX (Boston, 1885).
Walpole, Horace, *Memoirs of George III* (4 vols., London, 1894).
Wheatley, Henry B. (ed.), *The Historical and Posthumous Memoirs of Sir Nathaniel Wraxall, 1772-1784* (London, 1884).
Willard, Margaret Wheeler (ed.), *Letters on the American Revolution, 1774-1776* (Boston and New York, 1925).

## BIBLIOGRAPHIES AND GUIDES

Andrews, Charles M. and Davenport, Frances G., *Guide to the Manuscript Materials for the History of the United States to 1783, in the British Museum, in Minor London Archives, and in the Libraries of Oxford and Cambridge* (Washington, 1908).

# BIBLIOGRAPHY

Andrews, Charles M., *Guide to Materials for American History to 1783 in the Public Record Office of Great Britain* (2 vols., Washington, 1912-14).
——, *List of Commissions, Instructions and Additional Instructions Issued to the Royal Governors and others in America* (Washington, 1913).
*Burke's Peerage* (London, 1930).
*Dictionary of American Biography* (20 vols., New York, 1928-36).
*Dictionary of National Biography* (63 vols., London, 1885-1890).
Drake, Francis Samuel, *Dictionary of American Biography* (Boston, 1876).
Evans, Charles, *American Bibliography, 1639-1820* (Chicago, 1903).
Halkett, Samuel and Laing, John, *Dictionary of Anonymous and Pseudonymous Literature* (new edition, Edinburgh and London, 1926).
*Harpers' Encyclopaedia of United States History from 458 A. D. to 1912* (New York and London, 1912).
Haydn, Joseph, *The Book of Dignities* (London, 1894, 3rd ed.).
Parker, D. W., *A Guide to the Documents in the Manuscript Room at the Public Archives of Canada* (Ottawa, 1914).
——, *Guide to the Materials for United States History in Canadian Archives* (Washington, 1913).
Rivington, John, *The Court and City Register* (London, 1769-1783).
Sabin, Joseph, *A Dictionary of Books Relating to America from its Discovery to the Present Time* (New York, 1868-1936).

## GENERAL SECONDARY WORKS

Adams, R. G., *Political Ideas of the American Revolution* (Durham, N. C., 1922).
Aikin, John, *Annals of the Reign of King George the Third* (London, 1820).
[Almon, John], *Biographical, Literary and Political Anecdotes* ... (London, 1797).
Alvord, C. W., *The Mississippi Valley in British Politics* (2 vols., Cleveland, 1917).
Anderson, Troyer Steele, *The Command of the Howe Brothers during the American Revolution* (Oxford, 1936).
Andrews, C. M., *The Colonial Background of the American Revolution* (New Haven, 1924).
——, *The Colonial Period of American History* (4 vols., New Haven, 1934-38).
*Anecdotes of the Life of the Right Hon. William Pitt, Earl of Chatham* (London, 1797), I, 351-52 (note).
*Annual Register*, 1768, 1782 (London, 1769, 1783).
Anson, Sir Wm. R., *Law and Custom of the Constitution* (4th rev. ed., Oxford and N. Y., 1909).
Bancroft, George, *History of the United States* (Boston, 1834-75).
Basye, Arthur H., "The Earl of Carlisle and the Board of Trade, 1779," *American Historical Review*, XXII, 334 (Jan., 1917).
——, "The Secretary of State for the Colonies," *American Historical Review*, XXVIII, 13-23 (October, 1922).
——, *The Lords Commissioners of Trade and Plantations* (New Haven, 1925).

Batchelder, Samuel Francis, *The Life and Surprising Adventures of John Nutting Cambridge Loyalist and his Strange Connection with the Penobscot Expedition of 1779* (Reprinted from the *Proceedings of the Cambridge Historical Society*, Cambridge, 1912).
Brebner, J. B., " The Partition of Nova Scotia," *Canadian Historical Review,* XV, 57 (March, 1934).
——, " Nova Scotia's Remedy for the American Revolution," *Canadian Historical Review,* XV, 171 (June, 1934).
——, *The Neutral Yankees of Nova Scotia* (New York, 1937).
Brougham, Henry Peter, Lord, *Historical Sketches of Statesmen who Flourished in the Reign of George III* (London, N. D.).
Burt, A. L., *Imperial Architects* (Oxford, 1913).
——, *The Old Province of Quebec* (Toronto, 1933).
Campbell, Lord John, *The Lives of the Lord Chancellors and Keepers of the Great Seal of England, from the Earliest Times till the Reign of King George IV* (London, 1847).
Channing, Edward, *A History of the United States,* Vol. III (New York, 1924).
Clark, Dora Mae, *British Opinion and the American Revolution* (New Haven, 1930).
——, " The Office of Secretary to the Treasury," *American Historical Review,* XLII, 22-45 (October, 1936).
Coupland, Reginald, *The American Revolution and the British Empire* (London and N. Y., 1930).
Coxe, W. M., *Memoirs of Walpole,* Vol. II (new ed., 3 vols., London, 1800).
Curtis, Edward E., *The Organization of the British Army in the American Revolution* (New Haven, London and Oxford, 1926).
Cuvier, G., *Éloges historiques* (Paris, 1860).
Dickerson, O. M., *American Colonial Government, 1696-1765* (Cleveland, 1912).
Egerton, H. E., " Lord George Germain and Sir William Howe," *English Historical Review,* XXV, 315 (April, 1910).
Ellis, G. E., *Memoir of Sir Benjamin Thompson, Count Rumford* (Boston, 1871).
Evans, F. M. Greir, " Emoluments of the Principal Secretaries of State in the 17th Century," *English Historical Review,* XXXV, 526 (October, 1920).
Fitzmaurice, Lord, *Life of William Earl of Shelburne* (London, 1912).
French, Allen, *General Gage's Informers* (Ann Arbor, 1932).
*Gentleman's Magazine* (London, 1768-1810).
Gilroy, Marion, " The Partition of Nova Scotia," *Canadian Historical Review,* XIV, 375 (December, 1933).
——, " The Partition of Nova Scotia," *Canadian Historical Review,* XVI, 91 (March, 1935).
Graham, Gerald, *British Policy and Canada, 1774-1791* (London, 1930).
Guttridge, George H., "Lord George Germain in Office, 1775-1782," *American Historical Review,* XXXIII, 23-43 (October, 1927).

## BIBLIOGRAPHY 175

Hale, R. W., "Some Account of Benjamin Thompson, Count Rumford," *New England Quarterly*, I, 505-31 (October, 1928).
Hoon, E. E., *The Organization of the English Customs System, 1696-1786* (New York, 1938).
King, Charles R. (ed.), *The Life and Correspondence of Rufus King*, Vol. III (New York, 1896).
Lecky, W. E. H., *History of England in the Eighteenth Century*, Vol. III (New York, 1903).
——, *History of Ireland in the Eighteenth Century* (New York, 1893).
*London County Council's Survey of London*, Vol. XIV (London, N. D.).
McIlwain, C. H., *The American Revolution: A Constitutional Interpretation* (New York, 1923).
Manning, Mrs. Helen Taft, *British Colonial Government After the American Revolution, 1782-1820* (New Haven, 1933).
Martin, Chester, *Empire and Commonwealth* (Oxford, 1929).
Namier, L. B., *The Structure of Politics at the Accession of George III* (London, 1929).
——, *England in the Age of the American Revolution* (London, 1930).
Nichols, John, *Literary Anecdotes of the Eighteenth Century* (London, 1812-16).
Pemberton, W. Baring, *Lord North* (London, 1939).
Pownall, C. A. W., *Thomas Pownall, Governor of the Colony of Massachusetts Bay* (London, 1908).
Rose, J. H., Newton, A. P. and Benians, E. A. (eds.), *Cambridge History of the British Empire* (London and New York, 1929-36).
Sabine, Lorenzo, *Biographical Sketches of Loyalists of the American Revolution* (Boston, 1864).
Schuyler, R. L., *Parliament and the British Empire* (New York, 1929).
Tatum, E. H., Jr., "Ambrose Serle, Secretary to Lord Howe, 1776-78," *Huntington Library Quarterly*, II, 265-84 (April, 1938).
Thomas, F. S., *Notes of Materials for the History of Public Departments* (London, 1846).
Thomson, Mark A., *The Secretaries of State, 1681-1782* (Oxford, 1932).
Tyler, M. C., *Literary History of the American Revolution, 1763-1783* (New York, 1898-1900).
Van Tyne, Claude, *The Loyalists in the American Revolution* (New York, 1902).
——, *Causes of the War of Independence* (Boston and New York, 1922).
——, *The War of Independence: American Phase* (Boston, 1929).
Williams, Basil, *Earl of Chatham* (2 vols., London, 1913).
Williamson, Joseph, "The Proposed Province of New Ireland," *Collections of the Maine Historical Society*, VII, 201-06 (Portland, 1876).
Winsor, Justin (ed.), *Narrative and Critical History of America*, Vol. VI (Boston and New York, 1887).
Yorke, Philip C., *The Life and Correspondence of Philip Yorke Earl of Hardwicke, Lord High Chancellor of Great Britain* (Cambridge, 1913).

# INDEX

Adams, John, 129
Admiralty, 12. 14, 17, 59, 67-8, 69, 74, 84, 86, 88-9, 90, 91, 121, 122, 123, 124, 128, 162
Africa, 68, 71, 72, 79, 146
Agent, colonial, 56, 105
Albany, 149
Alleghanies, 149
Almon, John, 85, 136
American Colonies, 11-12, 20-1, 139, 140, 141, 142-43, 148-55
American (Colonial) Department, 20-1, 25-6, 27, 33-43, 48, 50, 51 2, 55-6, 58-60, 61 note 11, 68, 70-2, 73, 74-5, 86-95, 126-27, 147, 159, 165, 166
American Revolution, 50, 53, 54, 74, 75, 84-5, 88, 94, 95, 102, 104, 105, 148, 154, 166
American (Colonial) Secretary, 26, 27, 31 note 9, 36, 45 note 16, 48, 49, 50, 51, 52, 53, 58, 59, 60, 67, 70, 71, 79, 80, 83, 85, 93, 128, 136-37 154. *See also* Hillsborough, Dartmouth, Germain, Ellis, Third Secretary
Amherst, Lord Jeffrey, 87, 112, 123
"Ancient" Secretaries, 29, 55, 66, 70, 71, 73, 74, 137
Anderson, T. S., 106
Anne, Queen of England, 12
Antigua, 59
Atkinson, Richard, 123

Bahamas, 143
Barbados, 59, 60
Barré, Colonel Isaac, 140
Barrington, William, Viscount, 85, 86
Basye, A. H., 67, 80, 81, 82
Bath, William, Earl of, 16
Bavaria, 107
Bayard, Samuel, 56, 120
Beauchamp, Lord, 161
Bedford, John, Duke of, 13, 20
Bedfordites, 19
Bermuda, 92, 143
Bernard, Sir Francis, 137, 138, 144, 158 note 64
Bill (Economical Reform), 28, 159
Blackburn, John, 139, 140
Board of Customs, 59, 91, 121, 128, 151
Board of Ordnance, 86-8, 90, 91, 121, 122, 124

Board of Trade, 11, 12, 13, 14, 17, 18, 19, 26, 29, 33, 37, 39, 49, 50, 52, 59, 60, 67, 72, 75, 79-83, 100, 101, 121, 161, 165. *See also* Pownall, John
Boddington, John, 123
Boston, 87, 104, 138, 150
Buckingham, George, Earl of, 147
Buller, Charles, 41
Burgoyne, General John, 89, 106, 113, 114, 116, 127, 137, 141
Burke, Edmund, 17, 20, 28, 60, 83, 101, 103, 147, 159, 160, 161, 165, 166
Burke, William, 34, 50
Bute, John, Earl of, 15, 16

Campbell, Sir Archibald, 118, 143
Canada, 27, 30 note 3, 114, 122, 125, 127, 141, 143
Carleton, Sir Guy, 54, 74, 75, 113, 114, 116, 155
Carlisle, Frederick, Earl of, 82, 83, 164
Carteret, John, Earl Granville, 13
Cecil, Sir William, 12
Chamber keeper, 35, 51, 52, 62 note 21
Channing, Edward, 103
Charles II, 146
Cheke, Sir John, 12
Chester, Governor Peter, 93
Chesterfield, Philip, Earl of, 12, 18, 166
Church of England, 145, 151
Circular letters, 117
Clare, John, Earl of, 79, 80
Clark, George, 56
Clerks, 34, 37, 40-1, 42, 43, 51, 115
Clinton, Sir Henry, 89, 91, 94, 114, 116, 117, 125, 126, 142, 143, 144
Colonial, *see* American
Colonies, *see* American
*Comet*, the, 93
Commander in Chief, 55, 56, 68, 69, 71, 86, 115
Commissioners on Fees and Gratuities, 94, 126
Constitutional Act (Canada), 145, 151
Conway, General Henry, 19, 27, 34
Cooper, Sir Grey, 39, 139
Cornwallis, Charles, Marquis, 159, 162
Crown, 48, 50, 53, 60, 119, 149, 159

## INDEX

Cumberland, Richard, 34, 56, 82, 101, 106, 124
Cumberland, William Augustus, Duke of, 16
Cuvier, G., 107

Danforth, Thomas, 120
Dartmouth, William, Earl of, 17, 18, 19, 27, 36, 37, 39, 41, 48, 49, 50, 59, 67, 70, 72, 84, 100, 101, 111, 112, 113, 114, 121, 136, 137-38, 139, 141, 166
De Brahm, William, 118
D'Estaing, Count, 122
De Grey, Thomas, Jr., 28-9, 33, 35, 36, 38, 43-4 note 4, 100, 106-07
De Grey, Sir William, 36, 106
D'Oyley, Christian, 36, 37, 38, 39, 55, 100, 105-06, 107
Detroit, 57
Dick, William, 42, 55
*Diligence*, the, 93
Dominica, 40
Dundas, Henry, 162

East Florida, 145
Eden, William, 39, 72, 73, 74, 84, 106, 125, 154, 164
Edward VI, 12
Egremont, Charles, Earl of, 16
Elliott, Grey, 165
Ellis, Henry, 102, 103
Ellis, Welbore, Baron Mendip, 36, 100, 103, 162, 164, 167 note 23
Exchequer, 48

Falkland Islands, 68
Family Compact, 145
Fees, 40-1, 48, 49, 50, 51-5, 57, 60, 62 note 20, 63 notes 26 and 29
Fisher, John, 36, 37-8, 39, 41, 88, 100, 108, 165
Fishery Act, 147
Florida, 141
Fox, Charles James, 17, 160, 164, 165
Fox, Henry, 16
Fox-North Administration, 104
France, 88, 90, 141, 142
Franklin, Benjamin, 25, 29, 36, 41, 67, 136, 166
*Friendship*, the, 87

Gage, General Thomas, 54, 68, 107, 116, 117
Galloway, Joseph, 120
Gascoigne, Bamber, 72
*Gaspee* affair, 112

*Gazette*, the, 49, 84-5, 96 note 32, 117
George II, 13, 15, 16
George III, 15, 16, 17, 42, 54, 68-9, 70, 72, 73, 82, 103, 104, 112, 113, 137, 155, 159, 160, 162, 163, 165, 166
Georgia, 40, 55, 57, 58, 59, 60, 102, 103, 104, 116, 122, 123, 142, 143
Germain, Lord George, Viscount Sackville, 28-9, 34, 36, 38, 40, 42-3, 48, 49, 55, 58, 59, 60, 73, 74, 75, 82-3, 85, 87, 88, 90-1, 94, 100, 105, 106, 107, 111, 112, 113, 114, 116, 118, 119, 121, 122, 124, 125, 137, 141, 142, 143, 144-46, 148, 154, 155 note 10, 162-64
German mercenaries, 85, 122
Gibraltar, 32 note 10, 124
Gordon, Adam, 55, 56
Gower, Granville, Earl of, 66, 67, 82, 83
Grafton, Charles, Duke of, 19, 20, 21, 36, 160
Great Britain, 73, 150, 152, 153
Grenville, George, 15, 16, 19, 51, 103, 139, 140, 152

Haldimand, Sir Frederick, 54, 92, 114, 116, 117, 120, 125, 127
Halifax, George, Earl of, 13-14, 16, 17, 18, 21, 26, 80
Hardwicke, Philip, Earl of, 16
Henry VIII, 12
Herbert, Sir John, 12
Heron, Sir Richard, 147
Hillsborough, Wills, Earl of, 13, 17, 18, 20, 21, 25, 26, 27, 29, 33, 35, 36, 41, 54, 60, 66, 67, 68, 69, 80, 81, 87, 92, 93, 100, 101, 103, 119, 128, 137, 138, 149, 162
Holdernesse, Robert, Earl of, 14
Home Office, 35, 165, 166
House of Commons, 16, 18, 19, 28, 29, 36, 38, 40, 73, 90, 106, 111, 115, 125, 146, 161, 163
House of Lords, 29, 40, 107, 129
Howe, Sir William, 39, 54, 94, 105, 106, 113, 114, 116, 117, 119-20, 126, 143
Hughes, Richard, 145
Hughes, William, 60
Hutchinson, John, 34
Hutchinson, Thomas, 33, 49, 105, 106, 117, 118, 119, 120, 138, 144

Indian presents, 39, 56-7, 58, 64 note 42, 90, 91, 116-17, 122, 130
Indians, 40, 142, 149

# INDEX

Ireland, 70, 71, 75, 83, 104, 122, 130, 146-48, 153, 157 note 55, 160, 164
Jacobitism, 15
Jamaica, 59, 66, 93, 118
James I, 12
Jenkinson, Charles, 161, 164
Jennings, Richard, 129
Johnson, Colonel Guy, 89, 116
Johnson, William Samuel, 25
Justice of the Peace, 57, 129

King, Rufus, 107
King, the, see George III
King's American Dragoons, 107
King's College, New York, 52
King's Friends, 166
King's system, 16, 17, 20, 43, 159, 160, 161, 162, 166
Knox, John, 102
Knox, William, 33, 36, 37, 38, 39, 40, 51, 55, 56, 57, 58, 59, 60, 62 note 15, 64 note 42, 66, 72, 75, 79, 87, 88, 89, 90, 91, 92, 100, 101, 102-05, 106, 109, 111, 112, 113, 114, 115, 116-17, 118, 119, 120, 121, 122, 123, 124, 125, 126-27, 128, 129, 130, 136, 137, 138, 139-40, 141, 142, 143-45, 146-54, 155 notes 5 and 10, 163, 164, 165

Lake, Sir Thomas, 12
Larpent, John, 34, 35, 51, 55
Lavoisier, Antoine, 108
Lecky, W. E. H., 103
Leeward Islands, 92, 102
Legge, Francis, 113, 116, 120
Leicester House, 15
Leyborne, Governor W. L., 69
Lincoln, 101
Liverpool, 72
Lord Chamberlain, 42
Lord Lieutenant of Ireland, 75, 83
Loyalists, 38, 89, 107, 108, 109, 129, 142, 143, 145, 146, 151
Luttrell, Temple, 75
Lyttleton, Henry, 102

Maine, 144
Maryland, 151
Massachusetts, 107, 108, 137, 138, 144, 146
Mawbey, Sir Joseph, 28
Melcombe, George, Baron, 16
Messengers, 35, 41-3
Methuen, Sir Paul, 13
Mississippi, 142
Mitton, William, 35
Monk, James, Jr., 116
Montagu, Lord Charles, 60, 138

Montagu, Frederick, 59
Montagu lodgings, 33
Montreal, 57, 149
Mosquito Shore, 142
Muly, Elizabeth, 35, 51
Muly, Philip, 35

Namier, L. B., 15, 16
Navigation Acts, 104, 157 note 50
Navy Board, 89, 90, 124
Nepotism, 35-6
Nesbitt, William, 116
Netherlands, 81
New Brunswick, 104, 105, 146
Newcastle, Henry Holles, Duke of, 13, 14, 15, 16, 26, 28
New England, 142, 143
Newfoundland, 27, 87, 141, 143, 153
New Hampshire, 107, 108, 138
New Ireland, 143, 144-46, 148, 156 note 42
New York, 59, 92, 93, 104, 121, 122, 123, 138, 143, 150, 151
Niagara, 57
North Administration, 16, 66, 101, 109, 145, 162
North America, 68
North, Lord Frederick, 16, 22 note 23, 39, 58, 67, 68, 69, 71, 73, 75, 82, 85, 94, 103, 104, 112, 113, 125, 127, 137, 139-40, 142, 144, 146, 147, 148, 154, 158 note 62, 163-64
Northern Department, 13, 21 note 2, 25, 26, 30, 34, 36, 40, 42, 48, 49, 50, 52-3, 54, 66, 70, 74, 81, 83-5, 102, 107, 113, 121, 160. *See also* "Ancient" Secretaries
Northumberland, Hugh, Duke of, 12
Nova Scotia, 57, 113, 116, 143, 145, 156 note 23
Nutting, John, 156 note 42

O'Brien, Sir Lucius, 157 note 59
Oliver, Andrew, 118
Oliver, Peter, 145
Order-in-council (July 2, 1783), 104
Oswego, 149

Packet boats, 92, 93, 94
Pallister, Sir Hugh, 122
Palman, George, 35, 165
Parliament, 11, 33, 38, 51, 60, 139, 140, 145, 149, 151, 152-53. *See also* House of Commons, House of Lords
Patronage, 16, 58-60, 66, 77 note 17
Paymaster-General of the Forces, 12

# INDEX

Pelham, Henry, 15
Penn, William, 117
Pennsylvania, 151
Penobscot, 142, 143, 144
Pensacola, 57, 93
Pensions, 56, 58, 60, 104, 159
Pery, Edmund, 147
Petre, Sir William, 12
Phelps, Major Richard, 34, 36, 55, 62 note 14, 102, 103
Philadelphia, 125, 142, 143
Pitt, William, Earl of Chatham, 14, 15, 16, 18, 19, 20
Pitt, William, the Younger, 28
Place Acts, 18, 19, 23 note 29, 25, 27, 29, 106
Placentia, 87
Pollock, William, 34, 35, 40-1, 50, 51, 55, 120, 129, 165
Porten, Sir Stanier, 128, 146
Post Office, 51, 53, 92-4, 121, 128
Postmaster-General, 92, 93, 106
Pownall, George, 35, 102
Pownall, John, 33, 34, 35, 36, 37, 38, 41, 50-1, 55, 56, 57, 58, 59, 60, 64 note 47, 67, 69, 70, 72, 73, 74, 75, 80, 81, 82, 84, 90, 91, 93, 94, 100-02, 103, 105, 109 and note 1, 112, 113, 115, 116, 119, 122, 124, 128, 130, 136, 37, 138, 139, 154, 161
Pownall, John Lillingston, 35, 60
Pownall, Thomas, 11, 13, 17, 18, 35, 66, 80, 100, 162
Precis, 112, 125-27
Prevost, Major-General Augustine, 143
Prince Edward Island, 105
Privy Council, 11, 26, 29, 72, 80, 81, 84, 94, 121, 165
Proclamation (1763), 149
Proclamation (1775), 117
Provincial Corps, 88
Public Record Office, 51

Quebec, 57, 58, 75, 122, 127
Quebec Act, 114, 127
Queensbury, James, Duke of, 12, 21-2 note 6
Quit rents, 145

Rhode Island, 142, 143
Richmond, Charles, Duke of, 18
Riedesel, Major General Friedrich von, 118
Rigby, Richard, 162
Robertson, Governor James, 120
Robinson, John, 40, 60, 91, 92

Rochford, William, Earl of, 36, 39, 42, 59, 66, 67, 69, 70, 160. *See also* "Ancient" Secretaries
Rockingham, Charles, Marquis of, 15, 17, 18, 59, 164
Rodney, Admiral Sir George Bridges, 129
Roxborough, John, Duke of, 13
Royal Institution of Great Britain, 108
Rumford, Count, *see* Thompson, Sir Benjamin

Sackville, *see* Germain
St. Augustine, 57, 143
St. Croix, 144
St. Eustatius, 129, 135 note 105
St. John, 72
Salaries, 48-51, 53
Sandwich, John, Earl of, 16, 102, 113, 162
Saratoga, 106, 114, 127, 141
Savannah, 102, 104, 143
Sawer, William, 34, 35
Sawka River, 144
Scotland, Third Secretary for, 12-13, 26, 160
Seals, 26, 30-1 note 5, 49
Secretary of State, *see* American Secretary, Northern and Southern Departments, Third Secretary, "Ancient" Secretaries, Scotland
Senegambia, 27, 83
Serle, Ambrose, 34, 35, 51, 82
Seven Years' War, 15
Shelburne, William, Earl of, 18, 19, 20, 34, 38, 40, 41, 104, 108, 160, 164, 165
Sidmouth, Henry, Viscount, 41
Simpson, James, 116, 119, 131 note 26, 143
Sinecures, 55-6, 60
South Carolina, 57, 93, 102, 119, 138
Southern Department, 11, 13, 14, 18, 19, 20, 24 note 41, 25, 26, 30, 34, 36, 38, 42, 48, 49, 50, 52-3, 54, 58, 67, 68, 69, 70, 71, 74, 75, 78 note 44, 80, 83-5, 108, 113, 121, 128, 146-47, 160, 164, 165. *See also* "Ancient" Secretaries
Spain, 68, 88, 142
Stanhope, James, Earl of, 13
Stephens, Philip, 84, 122
Stormont, David, Viscount, 162, 164
Stuart, Colonel John, 120
Suffolk, Henry, Earl of, 16, 39, 40, 42, 54, 66, 68, 69, 70, 72, 73, 74, 75, 82,

INDEX                                      181

83, 84, 107, 112, 113, 160. *See also*
"Ancient " Secretaries
Superintendent of Indian Affairs, 52
Third Secretary, 12, 14, 18, 19, 25, 26,
    27, 29, 30, 33, 35, 49, 66, 67, 69, 73,
    74, 80. *See also* American Secretary, Scotland
Thompson, Sir Benjamin, Count
    Rumford, 36, 37, 55, 59, 88, 100,
    107-08, 129
Thurlow, Edward, Baron, 16, 127
Tories, 15, 16, 22 note 24, 145
Townshend, Charles, second Viscount (1674-1738), 13
Townshend, Charles (1725-1767), 16,
    17, 18, 28
Townshend, Thomas, 160
Treasury, 11, 14, 15, 17, 33, 38, 40, 50,
    56-7, 58, 59, 65 note 61, 89-92, 121,
    122, 124, 128
Tryon, Governor William, 112, 117,
    119, 138
Tweeddale, John, Marquis of, 13

Under-secretaries, 30-1 note 5, 35,
    36-40, 45-6 note 17, 48, 50, 51-2, 53,
    56-7, 58, 61 note 12, 82, 85, 91-2, 94,
    100-09, 111, 119-20, 121, 123-28, 132
    note 43, 136, 154, 165. *See also* De
    Grey, D'Oyley, Eden, Fisher,
    Knox, Phelps, Porten, Pownall,
    Thompson
United States, 104, 152

Upper Canada, 145

Vaughan, General William, 125
Victualling Board, 90
Virginia, 59, 66, 120

Walpole, Horace, 20, 162, 165
Walpole, Robert, 13, 15
Walsingham, Baron, *see* De Grey
War Office, 12, 67-8, 69, 74, 85-6, 89,
    91, 105, 121, 124
Wedderburn, Alexander, 16, 29, 30,
    73, 74, 125, 146
Wentworth, Governor Benning, 108,
    120
West Florida, 142
West Indies, 14, 27, 58, 59, 68, 79, 88,
    92, 104, 123, 124, 141, 143, 160
Weymouth, Thomas, Viscount, 36,
    54, 66, 67, 73, 82, 83, 112, 121, 146,
    159
Whately, Thomas, 118
Whigs, 15, 16, 159, 162
Whitehall, 33
Wilmot, Eardley, 35, 165
Wright, Governor James, 60, 116,
    117, 119
Wright, Sir Sampson, 129
Wynood, Sir Ralph, 12

Yorke, Charles, 16
Yorke, Sir Joseph, 84
Yorktown, 159, 163